MAKING WAVES

In recognition of his contribution
to the origin and birth of Greenpeace,
this book is dedicated to the memory of
Irving Stowe, (1915-1974).

MAKING WAVES

The Origins and Future of Greenpeace

Jim Bohlen

BLACK
ROSE
BOOKS

Montreal/New York/London

Black Rose Books No. DD295

Hardcover ISBN: 1-55164-167-4 (bound) Paperback ISBN: 1-55164-166-6 (pbk.)

Canadian Cataloguing in Publication Data

Bohlen, Jim

Making waves : the origins and future of Greenpeace

Includes bibliographical references and index.
Hardcover ISBN: 1-55164-167-4 (bound) Paperback ISBN: 1-55164-166-6 (pbk.)
1. Greenpeace International–History. I. Title

QH75.A1B64 2000   363.7'0577   C99-901583-4

Grateful acknowledgment is extended to the following for permission to reprint copyright material: to Greenpeace Canada, and to Robert Keziere for use of photographs.

Cover design by Associés libres, Montréal

C.P. 1258	2250 Military Road	99 Wallis Road
Succ. Place du Parc	Tonawanda, NY	London, E9 5LN
Montréal, H2W 2R3	14150	England
Canada	USA	UK

To order books in North America:
(phone) 1-800-565-9523 (fax) 1-800-221-9985
In Europe: (phone) London 44 (0)20 8986-4854 (fax) 44 (0)20 8533-5821

Our Web Site address: http://www.web.net/blackrosebooks

A publication of the Institute of Policy Alternatives of Montréal (IPAM)

Printed in Canada

The Canada Council | Le Conseil des Arts
for the Arts | du Canada

TABLE OF CONTENTS

INTRODUCTION

There is one thing stronger than all the armies in the world, and that is an idea whose time has come.　　—Victor Hugo (1893)

On September 15, 1996, the 25th anniversary of the first Greenpeace campaign, I was asked how the idea of Greenpeace came about, and, did I think, at the beginning, that it might grow into the world's most influential environmental organization. The short answer was no. At that time, we were focused on the one direct action in front of us. When we stood on the street corners of downtown Vancouver, wearing 'Ban the Bomb' sandwich boards, we were held together by personal commitment to stop nuclear testing.

As I thought back through my life, in search of a deeper answer, the importance, and the influence, of past events began to take hold. It was then, that the idea of this book came to me.

I had been making waves all my life. Some ebbed gently to shore, others tumbled back upon me with a frightening momentum. The best ones cascaded forward, rippled outward. I never knew, beforehand, which would be which, I only felt compelled to stir the waters.

I had started life in the 'Roaring Twenties,' in New York City. When I was three, the New York Stock Exchange crashed. The Great Depression was the background to my boyhood.

The United States entered World War II in December of 1941, the year generally considered to be the end of the Great Depression. I was fifteen.

Before long, I was seeing, firsthand, the devastation wrought by the nuclear bombs that had hastened the war's end. I was brought, inescapably, into a new age; once the bombs had been dropped, nothing would be the same. People were profoundly affected by the atomic bomb; they dug backyard bomb shelters and taught schoolchildren to dive beneath their desks.

After the war, a newly formed Federation of Atomic Scientists lobbied for control of atomic power to be shifted into civilian hands. Their efforts helped shape the Atomic Energy Act of 1946, which created the Atomic Energy Commission. But the AEC's creation was to raise as many problems as it answered.

I married, I pursued a career, I traveled, I had children.

An "iron curtain" descended through the middle of Europe, dividing Berlin; missiles steamed towards Cuba, chilling and frightening; the Korean War, the forgotten war, was fought; then, the Vietnam War, where young men died without the faintest idea why.

In my position as research scientist, I saw the direction in which we were headed and didn't like it. I moved my family to the relative safety of Canada. We protested the war and organized to receive draft-dodgers and war objectors.

The '60s were an exciting, revolutionary, turbulent time that brought radical changes to the country, but it was the 1970s—the anti-nuclear, anti-war, energy-starved '70s—that transformed it. It signaled the beginnings of a new public awareness of the environment, and, the impact of human development on it.

Oil shortages were the defining events of the 1970s. Thus began a rush to diversify our energy base and to reduce dependence on imported oil. The AEC broadened its nuclear horizons. In 1972, they held a series of public hearings on the topic. We challenged the nuclear industry demanding stiffer safety criteria.

I sought an alternative lifestyle, one that was ecologically appropriate. I invented energy self-reliant technologies. I entered politics.

Although it was not my first campaign of protest, from the moment the plan to confront the bomb was announced, the idea of Greenpeace was born. Motivated by the Quaker tradition of "bearing witness," we would set sail from Vancouver, to stop the nuclear explosion at Amchitka—in a halibut fishing boat. Her official name was the *Phyllis Cormack*, but within a very short time, she became popularly known as the *Greenpeace*.

What follows, in this book, is the long answer to the question, did I think, at the beginning, that that first Greenpeace action would became a dramatic focal point for an international movement. I enter into its writing with a deep sense of humility and appreciation. Over the years, thousands of people have worked for Greenpeace. Many have contributed substantial portions of their lives to shaping and building it.

Jim Bohlen
November 2000

Greenpeace founders: Jim Bohlen (1926-), Paul Cote (1948-), Irving Stowe (1915-1974).

Demonstration at Skagit River to prevent construction of High Ross Dam.

Jim, working on the media.

Closing the Douglas Peace Arch border crossing between the U.S. and Canada.

Original *Greenpeace* crew.

Greenpeace in Akutan lagoon, just waiting.

Wild and wonderful Aleutian Island scenery.

Williwaws, high velocity winds sweeping from the Bering Sea, over treeless terrain and funneled through mountain valleys, that whip the waves into frozen foam.

Greenpeace crew made honorary Kwagiulth at Alert Bay.

Greenpeace and *Greenpeace* Too at Union Bay.

Geodesic space-frame of laminated veneer lumber.

The geodesic dome where Jim and Marie lived while constructing their permanent home.

Jim and Marie's twin domes: one for cooking and eating, the other for relaxing and sleeping.

Solar greenhouse and shower.

Greenpeace Farm publications.

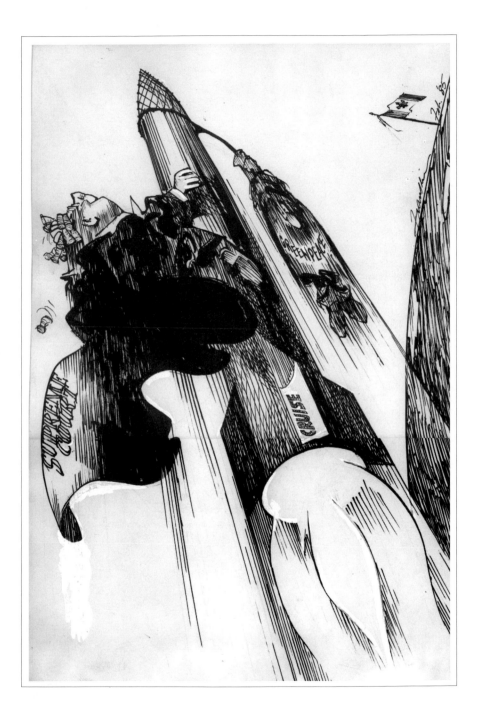

Globe and Mail cartoon of the Greenpeace Cruise Catcher.

Jim on speaking tour in the Okanagan.

CHAPTER 1

MAKING OF A RADICAL

I was born in the Bronx, New York City, on July 4th, 1926—one very hot and humid day (according to my mother), in a small private hospital on the corner of Kingsbridge Road and the Grand Concourse, across the street from the birthplace of Edgar Allan Poe.

Until 1930, we lived on Webb Avenue adjacent to the Kingsbridge Veterans Hospital. Most of the patients there were U.S. Army veterans, casualties of poison gas trench warfare during World War I. I recall riding my tricycle about the hospital grounds and often stopping to visit with the patients. My parents, my maternal grandparents, my aunt, her husband and myself, all lived together in a red brick five-story walk-up apartment house in a top-floor three-bedroom flat.

In October 1929, the stock market crashed. Father lost his job. My mother and my aunt were tenured staff secretaries in the New York City public school system; their job's were safe. My grandparents had no source of income to speak of. It was at this point that my father found work in Newark, New Jersey. He had to travel two hours to get to work, work a ten-hour day, then travel two hours to get back home.

Our next move was to Greenwich Village, close to Washington Square Park, on Waverly Place near the Arch. The rent was cheap; Grandfather Bohlen was superintendent to the apartment block.

Both of my grandfathers had led colorful lives.

My mother's father, Grandpa Sobernheim (for that was his name), was from Bingen am Rhine. His Jewish parents wanted him to become a rabbi. He became an atheist, and booking agent and manager, for a troop of midgets known as the Lilliputians. Up until he settled down at age 50, he and his charges roamed Europe, the highpoint of this career having been a special performance for the Tsar of Russia. After his career, he took a young Jewish woman from Bresslau for his wife. She gave birth to my mother and one set of fraternal twins. In New York City, in the 1930s, grandfather played chess in public parks for money. He was good at it; it became a source of income for the family. He also sold life insurance for the Metropolitan Life Insurance Company.

Grandfather Bohlen was an enormous man with enormous appetites, and, handsome to boot, bearing a striking resemblance to Franklin Roosevelt, his hero. Grandfather Bohlen came to the United States from Hungary, where he and his best friend had run from the military draft, and where his uncle, who encouraged him, was a reporter for the underground socialist press in Budapest. In New York City, he had lived in the Hungarian community located on the lower East Side—a tough, crime-ridden neighbourhood.

Grandfather was an extremely talented mechanic. In those days there were no college trained engineers. Creative work was initiated by the craftsman. Grandfather, when in Hungary, hand built racing cars for the Emperor Franz Josef and maintained his fleet of limousines and his private steam train. He could build entire automobile engines (circa 1905). It was this talent that got him to New York City, where he was employed on the Hecksher estate in Long Island, attending to that millionaire's limousines and race cars. After a few years there (he left due to personal 'trouble' with the boss), he went to work for the Brewster Corporation, in Newark, hand building patent leather covered aluminum limousine bodies on Rolls Royce chassis. And then came what would prove to be the worst mistake of his productive life (aside from his five marriages). He had met a somewhat weird inventor (Hungarian), who had ideas for hand-held electrically-powered tools—drills, and the like. My grandfather built the prototypes, and they showed them at a machinery exhibition where two entrepreneurs made the inventor and my grandfather an offer. Unfortunately, some sort of disagreement ensued; the deal with my grandfather fell through. Those two entrepreneurs turned out to be a Mr. Black and a Mr. Decker.

No kids my age lived at Washington Square Park. There were, however, great numbers of tramps sleeping in areaways and on park benches. One such, in conversation, told me he hadn't eaten in three days, so I invited him to our apartment. My mother wasn't home from work yet, but my aunt was, and made him something to eat.

I first went to school in the Village, at a privately operated kindergarten, there were no public ones; then, to public school in Rockville Center, Long Island. I lived at the home of my mother's best friend. It was while living in Rockville Center, that I got into my first spot of trouble.

I intended building an army of lead soldiers from molds I had gotten for Christmas, but I didn't have any lead. There was a construction site close by that did. I climbed over the high chain link fence, stuffed my pockets with lead, and started the climb back. I slipped and got tangled in the pointy part of the wire that protruded from the top of the fence. There I was, suspended upside down, pockets full of lead, the sun going down, getting colder by the minute. For obvious reasons I didn't cry out; I just hung there trying, every now and again, to get loose. It was only when the night watchman came on duty that I was discovered.

Soon after, I was reclaimed by my parents and went to live in an apartment near Yankee Stadium. There I attended the elementary school where my mother's sister worked. Midterm, my parents moved again. Over the next two years, I attended four different grade schools in the Bronx.

In the early 1930s Grandpa Bohlen and his wife of the time, Emily Jones, were unemployed, but had a few dollars of saved capital. They knew that people living and working the land were surviving the Depression much better than their urban cousins. They bought and moved onto a 40-acre abandoned, run-down farm in Sergeantsville, near Flemington, New Jersey (the place and time of the infamous Lindbergh kidnaping).

I was sent to the farm to live with my grandparents. My father's younger brother, Rudy, and his wife Harriet, had moved to the farm, as well, after they had lost their jobs in the city.

The two years living on my grandparent's farm was perhaps the best time of my childhood. I went to school in a one-room schoolhouse, with about 40 students—eight grades, all taught by one teacher. Every school day I walked three miles to and from the schoolhouse, weather notwithstanding. Along the way, kids from neighboring farms joined the little band wending its way to school. The process of learning and teaching, that went on in that one-room schoolhouse, was, in essence, an experience of cooperative sharing.

Grandfather and Uncle Rudy did a remarkable job of restoring the fertility to the once highly productive farm. It had been ruined by single cropping wheat, during World War I, when high prices year after year were enticing farmers to disregard good soil husbandry. Much of the topsoil had eroded off that hilltop farmland, resulting in gullies up to four feet deep and just as wide, extending for hundreds of feet. The family walked behind a tractor-drawn wagon picking up stones and tossing them in the gullies. Over several years, the gullies were filled. By following a prescribed crop rotation, and by adding soil amendments—phosphate and nitrogenous fertilizers—the topsoil was restored.

By the age of 10, I knew how to drive the tractor, doing the less critical tasks of discing and harrowing the soil, preparatory to planting. I warmed to the task, thrilled at the prospect of being a contributing member of the family.

Every Friday evening the whole family would go to the cellar beneath the house. There, in that cool place, the week's egg production was stored. Backlit by a candle, each egg was checked for blood spots or formation of embryos. The eggs were cleaned and packed in flats. At 4:00a.m. every Saturday morning, the flats were loaded into the Model A Ford pickup and we would make the trip to the Flemington farmer's market, about 12 miles away. The sale of these eggs, from about 150 laying hens, represented the family's only cash income.

Then, in 1938, my life suddenly turned in yet another direction; my mother took a sabbatical and her and I moved to Florida. For half a year I attended school in Miami Beach. When our time in Florida was up, I went to live with my father in Philadelphia—for the other half year. He had become an engineer after many years as a toolmaker. He was super handy, and could fix or build most any mechanical contrivance. We built gas-powered model airplanes together. We designed them, then found the raw balsa wood from which we cut out ribs and spars.

It was a good time; I came to know my father really well. I was old enough. School was another story. I had to struggle just to get through.

After Philadelphia, I moved back to the Bronx, to my mother. We lived on Clay Avenue, an older neighborhood. There, I met the Netzer family, avowed Stalinists. The Soviet Union could do no wrong. They tried hard to 'convert' me. I found it difficult to reconcile the professed 'humanism' of Communist doctrine. It didn't square well in view of the Russian invasion of little Finland. Nevertheless, I appreciated the Netzers, for they were warm generous people who considered me adult enough to debate aspects of social significance.

In those dark Depression days, where economic survival was shared by all, one would think it should have resulted in a common bond. Instead the community was sundered with strife. Teen-age gangs formed around ethnic backgrounds: the East Bronx Italians against the, unorganized, West Bronx Irish and Jews. They had no love for one another. The West Bronxites formed no gangs. Consequently, the Italian gangs often 'invaded' the West Bronx. They were resisted by *ad hoc* self-defense units of either Jewish or Irish origin. Being German / Jewish and Hungarian / Catholic, I joined no association. Eventually though, these 'associations' led to the formation of basketball teams and other non-violent diversions. However, the Italian gangs persisted every now and then. Their harassment consisted of surrounding a victim and 'pantsing' him down to his underwear, even in the coldest winter weather.

I managed to avoid suffering these indignities for two principal reasons. One, I was street smart from having so often been the new boy in town, and two, I would figured out the safe routes in advance. Plus, I could run like hell!

There were other kids my age who didn't want to be gang members either: Bill Tumarkin was one, and Morty Rubenstein another. Bill lived with his widowed mother, who could barely speak English. He was really down and hungry most of the time. I often took him to my apartment to share in what we had. Morty Rubenstein's mother, who was from the old Hebrew tradition, believed the fatter you were, the healthier you were. I was a string-bean. She was always putting food in front of me, but it was Bill Tumarkin who became the ultimate beneficiary of her largess.

War was an ongoing part of my young years. In the early 1930s the Japanese invaded Manchuria. After a bloody victory there, they struck China, where they engaged in the most horrendous practices against civilians. Most horrific was the rape of Nanking. I first learned of this from an illustrated bubble-gum card that depicted Japanese soldiers spearing Chinese babies on their bayonets. Even now, I dream of it.

In 1937, when I was 11, the Spanish Civil War erupted. The Lincoln Brigade was formed in the United States to engage the fascist forces of General Franco. The men who joined were mostly Communists, or at least sympathizers. In 1939, Hitler invaded Poland. Soon thereafter the Germans and the Soviet Union signed a mutual non-aggression pact. This further entrenched my distaste for the Stalinist regime.

While the U.S. didn't enter the fray until 1941, after the bombing of Pearl Harbor by the Japanese, a vigorous trade in war materials soon put an end to the Depression. Father, mother, uncle and aunt all got good paying jobs and moved away from the farm to be near their work. Grandfather and Emily were left to cope with running the farm, as best they could.

A Turning Point

In 1940, I celebrated my fourteenth birthday. I had just completed junior high school at P.S. 117 in the Bronx. After taking an entrance examination, I was accepted for matriculation at the Bronx High School of Science. My parents had lived apart for long periods of time during the Depression; that year they decided they wanted to live together once again, but my father's work was in Philadelphia, mother's in New York City. To resolve this situation, my mother gave up her job, and together, my parents bought a run-down farm in Bucks County, Pennsylvania. Of course, I had to leave the Bronx High School of Science.

The old stone house on the farm property was uninhabitable; it had to be restored and remodeled. During this interval, the family lived in an apartment in Jenkintown, a suburb of Philadelphia, some five miles from where my father worked, called Jericho Manor—several hundred apartments, in a two-story complex, nestled among tall trees.

I attended Abington High School. Barely 14, I was the youngest in my class. But, I did middlingly well, all things considered; my New York City junior high experience gave me a slight edge, for New York was acknowledged to have the nation's best public school system.

My high school years were during World War II, and it seemed that after every graduation exercise, the boys would enlisted in the Marines. Conversely, casualty lists grew longer every day.

One Christmas my parents gave me a Raleigh, three-speed, lightweight bike and I discovered a joy and freedom in bicycling that would stay with me the whole of my life. Since gasoline was severely rationed, highway traffic was light. I was able to ride my bike on every road—city and suburbs. My favorite destination, in downtown Philadelphia, was the Franklin Institute, a world class science museum. There they had workshops in optical space telescope lens grinding which I attended every Saturday morning, rain or shine.

I rode my bike all over Montgomery County. In the summer I cycled to the pool, where I would swim and watch the girls. I joined the stamp club, made the tennis team, and joined the aeronautics club, where I learned the elements of aircraft engineering under the guidance of Mr. Woodruff, a teacher I greatly respected.

In 1943, I graduated from Abington High School, and was accepted at the New York University School of Engineering. I prepped for an aeronautical engineering major at the Guggenheim School of Aeronautics there, at New York University. The campus was in the Bronx, not far from where I had been born in the Kingsbridge section.

The next year, I turned 18. I was inducted into the armed forces. I had previously qualified with the Navy's Radio Technician's program which enabled me to join the Navy with a rating of Seaman 1st Class, and was sent, along with about 200 others, to the Great Lakes Naval Training Center on Lake Michigan, 50 miles north of Chicago. When 'training' was completed, I was given a brief leave at home before I was sent to Stillwater, Oklahoma, there to attend electronic technician school. But once I understood it was to be a two-year stint, I dropped out.

By this time, the war in Europe was over; it didn't look as though I'd ever see action. I got reassigned to Radioman training at Madison, Wisconsin. Six months later, I graduated Radioman 3rd Class (the equivalent of Staff Sergeant in the army), and was assigned to a seagoing tugboat at Mares Island, California. Suddenly, I was headed for the Pacific Theater, to Okinawa, where Japanese pilots, trained to be human bombs, crashed their planes on the decks of warships.

But Okinawa fell.

Soon after, an order came through asking that all ship's crews be pared down to a minimum, and that the freed-up men be trained for active duty for a September invasion of mainland Japan. The Japanese were tenacious fighters; casualties were expected. I had just turned 19. It suddenly occurred to me, I might not make 20.

Then, on August 6th, 1945, the atom bomb was detonated over Hiroshima. On August 8th, a second bomb was dropped on Nagasaki. The war was over.

My ship, the USS Recovery, being a seagoing tug, had facilities onboard to salvage sunken ships, a capability much in demand after the war. Tokyo harbor was blocked by merchant ships that had been purposely sunk. We towed them away, opening up the harbor. After Japan, we went to Attu, in the Aleutian Islands where the Japanese garrison there was wiped out in a last ditch stand. There I learned how treacherous the seas could become in North Pacific Ocean latitudes, knowledge that would come in handy later in my life.

The Navy had a point system for qualifying the order in which naval personnel got demobilized. Age, marital status, and length of service got the highest priority. I was young, single, and had only been in for a short time, slightly more than one year. Consequently, I was one of the last to be discharged, almost one year after the war was officially over.

I, and millions of others, qualified for the GI Bill of Rights. This meant an expense paid four-year university education, so after my discharge, I went back to NYU, where I had already done my freshman year. Upon arriving, I found that due to the huge numbers of GI Bill students the capacity of the classes had been reached. I was told by the admissions department that I would be put on the waiting list; that perhaps in a year... This, after all I had been through, was unacceptable. I kicked up quite a fuss. Admissions folded; they simply set another place for yours truly. But the experience of college was uneventful, even boring: most of the class-work unrelated to the real world, and most of the professors had not yet entered the 20th century.

In A Family Way

I was married in June of 1948. I had just finished my junior year in college. My wife, Ann, an art student from nearby Allentown, came to New York, where she was prepared to work until I finished my studies.

During the previous two summers, I had worked for my father building aluminum truck bodies. He had built a factory on his farm. I liked the work, and I liked the cottage industry ambiance. Trouble was my father did not pay enough attention to sales, and, eventually, his venture failed. I had to find another job.

The factory stood empty, and the farm land, about 40 acres of cleared loamy soil, had lain fallow for several years. I got the bright idea of growing corn on this land and selling it to the Government's farm surplus purchase program. The farm machinery and implements had been inherited from the New Jersey family, so in May of 1948, I negotiated a rental agreement for the equipment, bought the seed, worked up the ground, and planted 40 acres of corn. In order to do this work I had to commute from New York to Doylestown every weekend for the months of April and May. I did the soil preparation and planted the entire crop. Then at the end of June, when classes were over, I spent the summer, cultivating and hand weeding the whole 40.

That year was better than usual for growing field corn. It was dry on the stalk, and ready for harvest middle of September, just before I was due to return to university. I contacted the Federal Agricultural Agency to make arrangements for them to pick up my crop. My plan was to run a truck alongside the harvester, and when full, deliver it to the Agency warehouse. But the local FAA told me they did not have sufficient facilities to hold all of the corn; I had to arrange storage somewhere else. This meant I had to rent or purchase steel silos. As well, to avoid rotting, the corn had to be of a low moisture content before it was put into a silo.

To get the desired moisture content I had to either harvest it all and store it loosely until it was ready for silage, or I could leave the crop on the stalk and let nature take its course. I had no alternative; I had to go to school. I harvested it all and temporarily stored it in my parent's empty factory/barn.

I shoveled 40 tons of corn from truck to barn, spread it over the barn floor, and when the moisture content was at the right level, I rented two silos, erected them, and shoveled the 40 tons of corn into the silos. I made no money. I did, however, learn a valuable lesson: farming, with an expectation of cash, was unreliable, to say the least.

Post University Experience

Upon graduation, as a mechanical engineer, in 1949, I found myself in a job market overcrowded with new engineering graduates. No more airplanes were awaiting design. A recession was in progress, no end in sight. I had married in my last year at university; I had family responsibilities, so I became a taxi driver in Manhattan. Eventually, I got a job as a draftsman for a firm where my father was the Chief Engineer. I didn't like the work, so after saving up some money, I took a sabbatical. My wife, Ann, and I, spent most of 1950 in postwar Europe.

We traveled by ocean liner, the *SS America*, landing at Southampton, England, then to London to visit a distant relative. London, in May, was so cold and damp that the bedsheets had to be warmed in front of the coal fire. A few weeks later, we were glad to be crossing the Channel, heading for springtime in Paris. After Paris, we went by train to Bremerhaven, Germany, where Ann's uncle was stationed in the army of occupation.

Germany was unrecognizable. Broken and burned locomotives and other rolling stock lay like stranded whales alongside the tracks. Rail stations, stood, their roofs gone, the skeleton-work of beams twisted and black, spanning the distance between opposite walls. Men, often wounded German soldiers, disfigured, waited for trains to take them who knew where.

The U.S. occupiers had commandeered, for their own use, every dwelling that was standing. To have access to food, the Germans worked as domestics; the families of the U.S. occupiers had plenty.

We traveled by bus from Bremerhaven, to bombed out Hamburg where we picked up the Autobahn and wove our way south covering the whole length of western Germany. Detours were numerous around bombed out bridges. Cities like Hannover, Kassel, Cologne, Bonn, and Frankfurt sustained heavy bomb damage, five years later, still very much evident.

We crossed the border into Switzerland at Basle, then to Montreux, on Lake Geneva. From there, to Nice and Cannes, in France, then west to Milan, Verona, Padua, and Venice. We turned south to Ferrara, Bologna, Ravenna, Florence, Perugia, Rome, Capri, Sorrento, and Naples. It was in Naples that we boarded the *Comte Di Biancamano* for the 12-day trip to New York City. And, it was onboard the *Comte Di Biancamano* where I danced with a young Italian actress by name of Sofia Loren.

Back in the U.S., the nation was in the throes of the Korean War. There were plenty of war related jobs requiring engineering skills, and some interesting new technologies were emerging. One was fiberglass reinforced plastics (FRP). To my delight, I was assigned to help set up a FRP laboratory to find applications in the trucking industry for this amazing new material. Before long I was known in the industry and, in 1954, was recruited by Lunn Laminates, a Long Island, New York company as a custom products sales engineer, with the assignment of finding large scale production opportunities. There I met, and got to know quite well, the engineer/futurist R. Buckminster Fuller. Among his many achievements Bucky designed the FRP geodesic radar domes that were deployed across northern Canada as an electronic shield to give early warning of a Soviet bomber attack from over the North Pole. My employer had successfully produced the prototype, but for political reasons was shut out of the bidding for the production run. Canada had entered into a pact with the U.S.—the Defense Production Sharing Agreement—construction of the production geodesic domes would be at the Liberty Aircraft Company, then, in Brantford, Ontario.

At my employer's request I made an exploratory visit to Toronto as a prospective engineering manager for the Canadian dome production. It was the dead of winter. The plane landed at the City Airport on Toronto Island, and from there, I went by cab to the Queen Elizabeth Hotel for the interview with Liberty personnel. The very low pay and the very low temperatures turned me off, quashing any further consideration of working in Canada.

As the Korean War lingered, showing signs of easing towards a permanent standoff, military budgets were cut. The company I worked for was doing about 80 percent of its business for the 'defense' industry. Management saw they would suffer a serious reduction in sales unless new markets were opened. After the geodesic dome project, I was assigned the job of sales engineer with the task of developing applications for FRP in the non-military sector.

Seeking civilian markets for defense related technology is often difficult. There is the matter of cost—most military production techniques are expensive and often not required in the production of civilian oriented applications—then, there is always some reluctance to change balanced by fear of losing ground to the competition. I had to find those most open to experiment and convince them to budget for the services which my company offered.

Sometimes a forward looking organization would seek new technology. In the FRP field this included General Motors production of the Chevrolet Corvette, and the Herman Miller company with the production of the FRP version of the Charles Eames chair. These were successful applications and are still being produced and used. My contribution was in convincing the United Parcel Service to develop a truck body that would be distinctive, rather than just another look-alike out of Detroit. The present day UPS local delivery trucks are of the same outward appearance as they were 40 years ago, still employing the original FRP design, yet retaining their distinctive appearance.

As techniques improved, other applications came to mind. A rather unusual innovation was the FRP burial casket. Casket manufacturers were looking for viable alternatives. A craftsman at the National Casket Company had the idea of substituting fiberglass reinforced plastics (FRP) for bronze. This idea caught on as bronze was expensive. A fiberglass look-alike, offered the same lasting qualities as bronze, but would cost a fraction of the price.

The casket company produced a few prototypes to test the market. In a short time, funeral directors across the nation wanted the fiberglass product. Unable to meet the demand themselves, the casket company wanted to contract my company. After doing a pre-production run, it was evident that my management was not thrilled with the prospect of continuing in the casket business.

I thought it a quite innocuous and harmless application of a wartime technology. Rather then abandon the project, I decided to approach the casket company with the idea that I would produce the fiberglass burial caskets. The casket company management liked the idea and basically financed me by advancing the sales price of the first 100 caskets.

In My Own Business

It was 1957, Sputnik had just flown, and I, at age 31, was launched into the milieu of manufacturing—without a life-preserver, and no knowledge of how to swim. I set up shop in Doylestown, Pennsylvania in my parents factory/barn—still empty.

The business experienced very high growth and its potential seemed unlimited. We had soon outgrown the barn and were looking for larger facilities. Other products were being considered for manufacture. Various housing to protect microwave antenna equipment from the elements was becoming popular. The catch to an expansion program was the immediate need for more capital investment.

A family friend, who was an investment counselor, advised that capital could be raised through a public stock offering. Having no experience at all in the financial markets, I had to trust the offering broker first in preparing the offer, and then in selling the stock. The broker I selected had a good track record in completing public offerings tailored to small business, so the offering was made public and we awaited the results. I even gave the broker a list of people who I thought might be interested in investing.

As I found out later, they were the *only* people the broker solicited. Together their investment made up about $75,000 of capital, out of the $300,000 named in the prospectus. Then, the originating broker said his firm was no longer interested in the stock and would cease trying to offer it. Meanwhile, we were spending the funds raised thus far on capital improvements. With no more capital coming in, we were cash poor and not able to refund capital already secured.

We had made a fundamental error with the stock offering. We had entered into what was called a "best efforts," when we should have entered into an "all or nothing" stock offering. This would have given the stock broker an incentive to sell the whole issue, for he would have received no commission until all of the stock was sold, and we, the offerer, would have received either the full amount or nothing. The consequences of this error was that we had to cease production, sell off whatever assets remained and distribute the proceeds to our suppliers and investors (and the bank). (A few years after our experience, the Security and Exchange Commission passed a law that made small business stock offerings of $300,000 or less, subject to a mandatory 'all or nothing' constraint.)

Radicalization

I never seemed to have much time to myself, what with the business, house projects, and attending to the needs of my two children. To find personal space I got into the habit of rising at 5:00a.m. 'to do my own thing.' It was at these times, that I would look for some concrete way to translate my emerging philosophy of life into an appropriate lifestyle.

I have always been an avid reader of Henry Miller's works. I was introduced to his writings while in Paris, during the early 1950s, where I purchased a copy of *The Tropic of Cancer*. This book was forbidden entry to the U.S.; I had smuggled it past the customs inspectors, hidden amongst the dirty laundry.

Miller is often trivialized by critics as simply a writer of 'dirty books.' I believe that Miller's smutty novels are, in places, a metaphor, which he used to gain notoriety. Most of his books (compared to what we see now) contain minimally 'offensive' verbiage, as for instance in the account of his trek across the United States: *The Air Conditioned Nightmare*. That book contained very little 'naughty' language.

I learned about the existence of Zen Buddhism from one of Miller's books. I tracked down a text entitled *Zen Buddhism*, written by Daitsu Suzuki, a Japanese ex-patriot monk/scholar. It is difficult to illustrate how the combination of Miller and Zen provided the stimulus for what was about to be a dramatic change in my way of thinking and acting. Nevertheless, I will try to explain, for much of what follows germinated from that paradigm shift.

Henry Miller was an expatriate American. He emigrated to France during the early 1930s. While living in Paris he met other American writers who, like himself, were self-exiled from the United States—deemed by them to be a cultural wasteland. Miller wrote on many subjects. His greatest contribution was a vigorous denunciation of middle-class materialist values. It should come as no surprise that everything Miller wrote was banned from entry to the United States.

His major thesis is that middle-class materialist values, if allowed to proliferate, will provoke the fracturing of the human community, and ultimately the extirpation of society. This was heady stuff for one already deeply immersed in the middle-class material culture, at a time (the 1950s) when middle-classness was next to godliness.

Zen Buddhism was mentioned by Miller as a religious practice that rejected materialism: Buddha was the son of a wealthy family who refused his inheritance and wandered about India's rural villages teaching the values of voluntary material simplicity as the path to Enlightenment. Zen Buddhism sprouted from Buddhist teachings when Buddhism crossed into China.There it evolved into Taoism. When Taoist teachings reached Japan, it surfaced as Zen Buddhism. These offshoots dealt with practical ways for the layperson to live a full and productive life while traveling the path towards Enlightenment.

Arising from the study of Zen was the awareness that striving for material success was counterproductive. Others have articulated similar ideas. Mahatma Gandhi is reported to have said: "There is sufficient for one's needs, but not for one's greeds." The Greek philosopher Horace wrote, 2000 years ago: "A man will always be a slave who does not know how to live upon a little." A more contemporary, Western version: "Live simply so that others may simply live." Integrating these philosophical and ethical constructs, attempting to weave them into an action-oriented lifestyle, would occupy most of my waking moments.

Times They Were A-Changin'

The various movements of the 1960s prepared the groundwork for a great revolution in human consciousness throughout the world. For me, it began in 1960 with the revelation that radiation from nuclear weapons atmospheric testing was polluting mother's milk with radioactive Strontium 90—an unconscionable tragedy.

The 1960s saw the Kennedy administration confronting Kruschev over the deployment of nuclear weapons rocket launch sites in Cuba; citizens building backyard bomb shelters, in case of nuclear attack; and the USSR, and the United States, rapidly building up nuclear deterrents of intercontinental ballistic missiles.

To defuse a growing anti-nuclear war movement, the U.S. Government trivialized the dangers of nuclear war by publicly advocating that you could protect yourself from being roasted alive during a hydrogen bomb attack by digging a trench, climbing in, and covering yourself with a door. "All you need," the saying went, "was a door and a shovel." Public schools held bomb protection drills. When the alarm was sounded, children would huddle under a desk; those outside, under parked cars. That our children were being asked to take part in this futile exercise, angered me.

In truth, no one really knew, nor seemed to care, what would actually take place in the event of a nuclear attack. Under some pressure from citizen's, our local government authorities agreed to investigate what a nuclear attack really meant. I volunteered to find out and was sent to a university campus near Jacksonville, Florida, where a civil defense workshop, related to nuclear war, was being conducted. The first thing they did was a slide show presentation of Hiroshima and Nagasaki survivors: ghastly photographs, the horror of which has never left me. To be aware that the U.S. was planning to accept casualties of this nature to be visited on our children was simply unacceptable. The rest of the seminar, which I refused to attend, dealt with rationalizations as to the effectiveness of the 'door and shovel' approach to a nuclear defense strategy.

This attitude disgusted me, but it also determined me to actively oppose nuclear weapons of mass destruction until they were wiped off the face of the Earth. On the face of it, I was undertaking a Quixotic lifestyle, jousting at windmills—knowing full well I had family responsibilities and few cash reserves.

Day after day I beat the bushes for work as an engineer in my field of fiberglass reinforced plastics. After several months my search led to the Hercules Powder Company in Rocky Hill, New Jersey, 30 miles from my home. They were recruiting an engineering staff to design and build components for guided missile rocket motors that involved the use of reinforced plastics.

I took the job, reservations about working on military rocket technology, not withstanding.

The U.S. Government gave tax breaks to military suppliers for research work done on finding civilian applications to war-related technologies. I was assigned to head up a small group of engineers and technicians with the purpose of creating new non-military applications for the unique process developed for use in constructing rocket motors.

A Budding Activist

All over the world, the anti-nuclear movement was picking up adherents and tactics were moving from simple demonstrations to non-violent direct action. The first, headed by Nobel Laureate Bertrand Russell, the philosopher/mathematician, occurred at Aldermaston, England. Then, a think tank, concerning nuclear matters, was established at Pugwash, near Halifax. There, the most influential nuclear physicists gathered periodically and reported their nuclear armaments concerns in a publication called *The Bulletin of Atomic Scientists*.

Protests in Philadelphia fostered an outreach to smaller population centers. The Quaker community in Doylestown, Pennsylvania, where I lived, organized local area demonstrations in solidarity with the Aldermaston march. I joined with a small group of mostly Quakers who regularly picketed at the Philadelphia City Hall with signs and petitions demanding an end to nuclear testing in the atmosphere. It was on one such demonstration that I met my second wife, Marie. She and I had attended the same high-school, though she had been one year ahead of me. I had gone to college right after graduation, then I served in the Navy for some years, so we had not met again until 1957, when I moved to Doylestown and started up my business.

On our birthdays, July 4th (Marie and I shared the same birth date), 1964, we were married. In our Volkswagon van, we went to Lake George, New York, camping. The Justice of the Peace who married us, had a son who was just leaving for active duty in Vietnam. This was a fitting reminder of an escalating, unacceptable war.

As the U.S. became bogged down in Vietnam, the Government looked to the development of ever more destructive conventional weapons; work at Hercules was becoming increasingly onerous. I became involved in the development of an anti-personnel shoulder-fired rocket. The warhead was made of small bits of razor blades calculated to make wounds difficult, if not impossible, to treat. These razor rounds, as they were called, would penetrate deep into the flesh—a real weapon of terror.

Hercules was asked by the military to develop the basic rocket launcher. The civilian application oriented facilities and personnel, with which I was associated, were ordered to put their work on hold and form a team to develop the rocket launcher. I refused. The writing was on the wall. In 1965, I quit.

The Greening

Marie and I shared an intense interest in nature; we joined the Sierra Club.

In the 1950s, the Delaware River, which separates Pennsylvania from New Jersey, overflowed its banks flooding land and buildings. Hurricane Hazel had been the cause. To correct the situation, and in an effort at preventing a recurrence, a plan was laid to pump 'surplus' water, from the river upstream, into an enormous artificial lake. The water would be stored and later released, as required, to control the flow of the river.

The lake's construction called for the inundation of thousands of acres of beautiful, and fertile, land, and the drowning of thousands of acres of eastern hardwood forest. And too, the downstream effects on fish migration would be disastrous.

The Sierra Club mounted a campaign to halt the pumped-storage project. We joined in. We collected petitions and wrote letters. Though not as direct an action as we would later introduce with Greenpeace, the campaign worked; the plan was shelved.

Protesting the Vietnam War

Our first taste of large scale anti-war demonstrations was early in 1964, in New York. We had come to the city on business, strolling along Central Park South, when we saw a line of people carrying placards marching down 5th Avenue. Our favorite pediatrician, Dr. Spock, had been raising the cry of the anti-war movement. We joined the march, elated, both by the prospect of contributing to the anti-war effort, and by being in the company of like-minded souls.

During 1965, and 1966, we took part in many anti-war rallies. Marie, and her mother, had joined the hundreds of thousands on the Mother's March to Washington. Another time, again in New York City, we were part of a line of protestors that stretched from the Central Park area known as Sheep Meadow, across the full width of 5th Avenue, and south to the United Nations Plaza, in front of the United Nations building. And, we were in good company: Martin Luther King, Stokely Carmichael (head of Students for a Democratic Society), and a host of young men burning their draft cards.

The USA: Love It or Leave It

Marie's son Paul graduated from high school in 1966. As long as he continued in school, he was eligible for a student draft deferment, but when he completed his studies, or if he dropped out, he would be drafted.

Paul told us that if he were called to serve, he would go to Canada where they had no draft and no law that would compel draft-dodgers to return to the United States. If the Vietnam War were to drag on, my own son, Lance, would have become eligible. Marie and I decided that neither of our boys would go to Canada alone.

Leaving the USA

As was my habit, I researched Canada at the library. Vancouver and Charlottetown looked to be good choices, but I had read about the mild winters of British Columbia, and decided on the better climate. In early April 1967, I booked a flight to Vancouver to explore the possibilities.

I was overcome by Vancouver's breathtaking beauty: by the flowering trees that lined Granville Street, all the way to English Bay, by the snow covered mountains, that loomed across the water.

I had made a tactical error when coming through Customs and Immigration, in having answered, honestly, when the immigration officer asked me what my purpose was in coming to Vancouver. Apparently, it was not permitted to come to Canada to look for work; one either already had a job in Canada, or was simply coming to visit. In any event, I was told I had four days.

Knowing virtually nothing about Vancouver, I had to carefully allocate my time. First on the agenda was where to look for work. Here I was, an unemployed mechanical engineer with 17 years of experience and no references. I had my diploma and copies of the few professional journals where my work was reported.

I wandered through the lumber yards along the Fraser River. Perhaps this industry could use my experience. But I did not want to get into industry, I wanted to do research. I visited the University of British Columbia; I wondered if they were doing research on wood products. I had an idea that my work in reinforced plastics would find a place in the wood research spectrum—the physical properties of wood and structural plastics were similar. I learned that UBC had no wood research work underway, but the Federal Government operated a forest products laboratory on campus. There I was granted an interview with the Director and the head of the wood engineering department. Two hours later, I had a job. They would even pay for the move.

This unanticipated good luck was followed by another. Intending to emigrate soon with my family, I needed to find a place for them to live—for Marie and myself, three children, two dogs and quite a few plants. A house, ideally, near to where I was to work.

I figured I had two days; it took five hours. So, there it was: in the course of three days, I had found an excellent, though low paying job, and, an affordable, though older, house, well located on a treed street.

The Draft-Dodger Movement

The diplomatic relationship between the United States and Canada includes a stipulation that any individual coming to either country is obliged to obey the laws of that country. And further, while in the country, an individual could not be punished for crimes committed in their native land unless those crimes were mutually recognized. There were exceptions, but Canada does not draft men into her armed forces, so legally resident emigrants to Canada would not be extradited to the United States for draft evasion. Draft-dodgers were accepted in Canada as political refugees, in that they would face persecution for draft-dodging if they were to return to the U.S. They were, therefore, eligible for legal immigrant status on the basis of humanitarian grounds.

With the Vietnam War still very much in progress, and escalating, more and more draft-dodgers were coming to Canada. Vancouver was the destination point for the west coast draft-evaders and deserters. An organization needed to be formed to assist these, often desperate, young men. Amy Dalgleish, Tony and Bob Bacon, and Marie and I, formed the Canadian Assistance to War Objectors (CAWO).

We established a string of safe houses where incoming draft-dodgers would be given bed and board for a few days, or, until they had found their own way around the Vancouver scene. For more than a year our house always had one or two; it was not an easy time for the family. Many of these young men had been condemned for making the move to Canada; there was a certain amount of shame in being a 'draft-dodger'—a hint of cowardliness, of shirking one's duty. But as the Vietnam War became prolonged, there were fewer and fewer draft-dodgers, and more and more war objectors. Anti-war sentiment was heightened; each year the organization, End the Arms Race, sponsored demonstrations. At one of these demonstrations, Marie and I met Dorothy and Irving Stowe. The Stowes were fellow emigres to Canada from the U.S., by way of New Zealand, where they had lived for several years. They, too, became involved with the CAWO.

By 1968, the war in Vietnam was not going well: Lyndon Johnson announced that he would not run again; Bobby Kennedy and Martin Luther King were both assassinated. Millions of people were in the streets clamoring for an end to the hostilities. Richard Nixon was elected President of the United States.

The draft-dodger movement trickled. Anti-war servicemen were joining the draft-resistance movements. The U.S. draft officials decided to defused the growing militancy of the movement by reclassifying most resisters 1-C, a virtual guarantee that holders of that classification would not be called to serve in the armed forces. Many draft-dodgers living in Canada went home.

Greenpeace is Conceived

When Marie and I left the United States, we had notified the Sierra Club that we were moving to Canada, but wanted to keep our membership in the Club. Because all of the Sierra Club activities were U.S. oriented, they did not have any Chapters outside of the U.S. In order to keep our membership, we were considered to be a part of the Pacific Northwest Chapter, with headquarters in Seattle, and were expected to attend meetings there. We asked the San Francisco head office for a list of members who, like us, were resident in British Columbia. We were surprised to learn that about 60 people were 'at large' members.

Terry Simmons, a young teaching assistant in Geography at the new Simon Fraser University held an organization meeting in September of 1969. It was attended by about 30 Club members. We agreed to formally organize as the Sierra Club of British Columbia, and filed the necessary papers. The Sierra Club of B.C. grew rapidly, for there was no activist organizations in British Columbia that were taking on tasks relating to ecological preservation.

Direct Action

About a year before the Sierra Club of B.C. was organized, I experienced my first, personal, direct action. The laboratory where I worked was adjacent to the University of British Columbia, a short distance from the Georgia Strait. Directly overhead was the Pacific flyway which saw thousands of north/south migrating birds in spring and fall. Outside the laboratory was a large old-growth western red cedar alive with migrating birds, resting. One sunny day, in the spring of 1969, I was sitting under that tree, eating my lunch, when a man, wielding a chain saw, approached. He asked me to move; he needed to cut down the tree in order to make a room for a temporary trailer addition to the laboratory. I was appalled. Not knowing what else to do, I stood up and spread-eagled myself, with my back against the tree trunk. I told the logger, somewhat passionately, this tree will *not* be cut down. The logger was so startled by my behaviour that he retreated.

News of this event spread quickly around the laboratory, and, ultimately, to the attention of the Director. I was called into his office. He wanted to know what on earth had prompted me to take such unusual action. I told him, as best I could. He let the incident pass, but warned me that another such exhibition would result in a written reprimand placed in my employment dossier.

Sierra Club drives, to increase membership, drew people into the organization who were leaders in the *ad hoc* groups that seemed to be springing up everywhere. The Cypress Bowl Committee was dealing with the destruction of old growth forests in West Vancouver, happening in order to make way for a ski development. The head of that group, Ken Farquharson was elected the first chairperson of the Sierra Club of B.C. I was the conservation chairman. We had also attracted Bill Chalmers, an organizer of the Save Wreck Beach Committee. This group was trying to prevent a four lane highway from being bulldozed around pristine Wreck Beach.

Citizens actions were successful in preserving a large portion of Cypress Bowl, and the Wreck Beach highway project was stopped by a sit-down in front of the bulldozers. The road around Wreck Beach was never built.

The first Sierra Club action occurred when the well known sculptor, Robert Smithson, proposed paving over a rocky islet at the mouth of Nanaimo Harbor with broken glass stuck with glue onto the rocky surface. This was to be a tourist attraction. A supine Government wasn't raising any objections. But this islet was home to seagulls. We could just imagine those birds cutting up their feet in the process of nesting on top of the broken glass. A reporter from the *Vancouver Sun*, Moira Farrow, did an op-ed piece, drawing attention to our concerns. The project was canceled. We had tasted our first victory, and, incidentally, the potential power of the press.

The next Club-sponsored action, under the name of the ROSS Committee (Run Out Skagit Spoilers), was an attempt to prevent the construction of the High Ross Dam, which would have backed up the Skagit River far into southern British Columbia. The dam was to increase electrical power for the U.S. Pacific Northwest. This campaign engaged the U.S. Sierra Club. The joined forces defeated the dam proposal. More and more members joined the Sierra Club of B.C.

We had learned that the Island of Amchitka in the Aleutians was being used as a nuclear testing site. Several bombs of relatively low yield had already been tested. The island was also in the heart of a Federal Wildlife Reserve. Eagles, peregrine falcons, and the endangered sea otter were amongst the protected animals.

Without any opposition, on October 2, 1969, the U.S. set off a 1-megaton nuclear bomb 1,200 meters (4000 feet) beneath the surface of Amchitka. On the day before the blast, code named Milrow, 2,000 protestors blocked the Douglas Peace Arch border crossing between the U.S. and Canada to demonstrate their outrage. A banner reading 'Don't Make a Wave. It's Your Fault if Our Fault Goes,' was placed at the Peace Arch, on the border between British Columbia and Washington State. 'Don't Make a Wave' alluded to a 1964 tidal wave that smashed ashore along the west coast, killing 115 people in Alaska and causing millions of dollars worth of property damage from British Columbia to California.

This tidal wave was produced by an enormous earthquake, centered in the Aleutians, registering 8.3 on the Richter scale. For 18 months thereafter, there were thousands of aftershocks.

Don't Make a Wave Committee

The majority of the protesters were students at the University of British Columbia and at the Simon Fraser University. These were the days of the student free speech movements. UBC had recently been visited by Jerry Rubin, who created a rebellious mood.

Student leaders articulated the unrest and sought targets for expressing the collective discomfort. They formed the shock troops of the anti-nuclear testing movement. Among them was a law student from West Vancouver, who had just returned from doing some post-graduate work at a Paris university. His name was Paul Cote. While there, he had been beaten by the French police. He was an innocent bystander, sipping an aperitif at a bistro frequented by students when the police charged, batons flailing. This had been a move by the Government of France to strike a blow against followers of Daniel Bendit Cohen, a leader of the French Student Free Speech Movement. Paul Cote had been radicalized; he was one of the organizers of the Milrow protest that closed the border at the Peace Arch.

Perhaps the most curious outcome of that protest had been the absence of coverage by the United States media. The closing of the border was an historic event. Not since the War of 1812 was the border between the USA and Canada closed, for even a moment, yet, the only media report was a small one-paragraph mention on the inside pages of the *Seattle Post Intelligencer*.

Soon after the Milrow underground test, the U.S. Atomic Energy Commission announced plans for a 5-megaton explosion named Cannikin. This test was scheduled for the autumn of 1971.

As conservation chairman of the Sierra Club, and with the approval of the B.C. Sierrans, I contacted Paul Cote and asked him to join us in

planning a campaign. I also talked my friend Irving Stowe into joining the
Sierra Club, for I was appreciative of his dedication to the anti-nuclear
cause, and his public relations, and fund-raising, abilities. The three of us,
the troika, set about planning for a Sierra Club campaign against
Cannikin.

Since, strictly speaking, our anti-Cannikin campaign was not a Sierra
Club initiative, we decided to form a totally independent group: on
November 28, 1969, the Don't Make a Wave Committee (DMAWC) was
born.

Long hours and several months elapsed with little agreement upon a plan
of action. The media showed little interest in reporting on an event that
wasn't scheduled to occur for almost two years. Paul Cote doubted
whether the students could be re-energized in sufficient numbers to block
the border again. We simply ran into a dead end in the idea department.

Then, one day in February 1970 (the 8th), as Marie and I sat over
our second cup of coffee, me pouring out my frustrations over the
Cannikin campaign, Marie looked and me and said, matter-of-fact: "Why
not sail a boat up there and confront the bomb." A wild idea!

Apparently, in 1952, the Quakers had planned to sail a ship, the
Golden Rule, out into the Pacific towards Eniwetok Atoll, where they
were to 'bear witness' to an atmospheric hydrogen bomb test. The *Golden
Rule* never made its destination; the crew was arrested, and the ship
impounded by the Coast Guard.

As we were discussing how we might conduct a similar protest
voyage to Amchitka, the phone rang. It was a reporter from the
Vancouver Sun checking up on various Sierra Club campaigns. Before I
knew it, I was laying out plans to go to Amchitka in a boat—to confront
the Bomb!

The next day, February 9th, the story (with only a few wrong
facts—this protest was neither sponsored, nor, sanctioned by the Sierra
Club), hit the headlines: *Sierra Club Plans N-Blast Blockade.*

Sierra Club Plans N-Blast Blockade
The VANCOUVER SUN: Mon., Feb. 9, 1970

A B.C. Conservation group said Sunday it hopes to charter a boat to blockade the next nuclear blast on Amchitka Island in the Aleutian group off Alaska.

Jim Bohlen education officer of the Sierra Club of B.C., said the group hopes to take a boat within the 12-mile limit of the island before the blast.

"And if the Americans want to go ahead with the test, they'll have to tow us out," he said. "Something must be done to stop the Americans from their insane ecological vandalism."

Bohlen said that if the boat were taken out of the immediate area, it would stay within the 30-mile limit to take measurements of possible radioactive fallout.

'NO DATA'

The blockade is designed to protest the U.S. Atomic Energy Commission's decision to conduct further nuclear tests in the Aleutians, and the lack of information received by Canada on the Oct. 2 initial blast on Amchitka.

The next explosion on the island will be three times as powerful as the 1969 blast, but the scheduled date has not been made public.

Bohlen said that according to the nuclear test ban treaty, underground atomic explosions are permitted as long as no radioactive fallout drifts across the borders of another country.

"Prior to last year's blast, the Americans promised to give all relevant data to the Canadian Government, but they never did," he said. "Now we want to find out, just how much these blasts affect us."

Bohlen said his group believes that a certain amount of fallout is drifting across the border into Canada and it wants to check this.

CITES PRECEDENT

A good-size fish boat would be adequate for the trip which, he said, is expected to take about 12 days.

Bohlen said the journey has a historical precedent. In 1952 during the first hydrogen-bomb tests at Bikini Atoll, a boat manned by Quakers and other pacifists blockaded the area.

"The publicity which they got was an initial factor in the test ban treaty," he said.

Bohlen said that one problem is that the date of the blast has not yet been announced publicly.

"However, we will contact (External affairs Minister Mitchell) Sharp to see what has been done in the past about notification," he said.

ENLISTS SUPPORT

Bohlen and the Sierra Club of B.C., with about 200 members, has not yet sought or received endorsement form the U.S. branches of the club.

Support will be enlisted, he said, from other conservation and anti-pollution groups, university students and the public.

"We will try to mount the most massive campaign ever, against this mad venture, and we'll make sure the American public is aware of how Canadians think about this matter," he said.

Bohlen said many U.S. government officials told him following the October blast that they had not been aware of any Canadian efforts to stop the test.

Bohlen added that the campaign will be conducted under the slogan 'Don't Make a Wave.'

Everybody thought we were crazy! To attempt a campaign of such magnitude! We had no money, no boat, and no idea of where to find one. Nonetheless, the campaign got underway. Irving and I, along with our respective families, spent weekends pitching the DMAW Amchitka campaign on the streets of Vancouver. We wore sandwich boards with 'Ban the Bomb' on the front, and a petition on the back which demanded that the Canadian Government carry a message to the U.S. authorities about the potential dangers of testing 5-megaton bombs on Amchitka. The public response was gratifying, but we weren't accumulating funds. We needed some kind of breakthrough.

Several people, mostly from the Sierra Club, joined with us in planning the campaign. The DMAWC called a meeting on February 24, 1970, which was held in the Fireside Room of the Vancouver Unitarian Church. The principal reason was to come up with a name for the campaign, and consequently, for the boat. Many suggestions were offered, but none seemed right. As the meeting threatened to draw to an end without any resolution in sight, someone, appropriately, offered the word 'peace.' Someone else said 'green' ought to be considered. Then, Bill Darnell, a Sierra Club member and an organizer for the Company of Young Canadians put it together. "Obviously," he said, "it has to be a *'green peace.'* "

Not bad, for "a group of hippies congregated in a damp church basement."

CHAPTER 2

CONFRONTING THE BOMB

Marie, being the artist of the committee, volunteered to make the green peace sign to be deployed on the boat. Her son Paul, an art student, agreed to design a logo for a lapel button. Irving and I would put up the $250 for the first 200 buttons that others agreed to distribute as a fund-raiser.

The button was to be one-inch in diameter, to include the peace symbol, the ecology symbol, and the words 'green' and 'peace.' With very little space to work with, Paul was having a problem keeping 'green' and 'peace' separated, when it occurred to me—why bother. Run the two words into one. The term 'Greenpeace,' as a one-word expression, thus came about quite by accident.

Irving had a genius for fund-raising. He came up with the idea of a benefit concert, to be held in Vancouver. Joni Mitchell, born in Saskatoon, Saskatchewan, was then at the top of the charts, and, she had never appeared in person, in Canada. When Irving learned of this, he convinced Joni's manager she should do the Greenpeace benefit. They agreed upon October 16, 1970. With this commitment in hand, Vancouver Coliseum, which held 10,000 people, was booked. Along with Joni Mitchell, Irving also got Phil Ochs, the famous anti-war folk-singer from the U.S., and the, then popular, local band Chilliwack.

At first ticket sales were slow, but as the concert day approached sales picked up and, in the end, we sold out. We were not sure why, until word had come that Joni was bringing along the brand new singing sensation, James Taylor.

The DMAWC netted about $17,000 from the concert. It would have been $3,000 more if the City, which owned the Coliseum, had not allowed the Pacific National Exhibition people to take a cut off the top. Considering that all the participants were volunteers, this left a bitter taste. But we rallied, as we believed we had the funds to secure a boat.

Neither Irving, nor I, had a clue as to where to look for one; Paul Cote provided the solution. From his extensive contacts amongst boat owners, he located one who proved willing to charter his vessel for the planned campaign against the bomb. His name was John Cormack, and he owned and captained an old halibut packer that was occasionally chartered by Federal Fisheries for their salmon tagging program. Paul was concerned about the condition of the boat, the *Phyllis Cormack*, but he had confidence in the seafaring abilities of the Captain, John Cormack. John had 40 years of experience halibut fishing in the stormy North Pacific Ocean.

We had applied to be registered as a nonprofit corporation, and on October 5, 1970, just prior to the Joni Mitchell benefit concert, we received official confirmation. A few months after the concert, Paul, Marie, and I met with Captain Cormack to sign a contract and define the terms and conditions of the charter: briefly, we paid $12,000 in advance, and, in return, John would engage and pay for an engineer to care for the mechanical aspects of running the boat. We would provision the vessel and pay for all of the fuel. The duration of the voyage would be six weeks. The DMAWC would not put the *Phyllis Cormack* at risk from impoundment. John Cormack would be in charge, with full decision-making regarding the operations of the boat. Direction as to destination, and authority to select the 'passengers' crew, was the responsibility of the DMAWC.

At this point, Paul told us that he had to pull back his day-to-day involvement in committee matters in order to concentrate on his studies, and, in order to get ready for his participation in the Olympic trials for the Soling class of racing boats. He did agree to go along on the Amchitka voyage providing it didn't interfere with the Olympic trial dates. Irving was never scheduled to sail; he suffered from a variety of physical disorders. That left me as the only one of the original founders of the DMAWC who would be on the crew of the protest boat.

On March 15, 1971, we called a press conference announcing that a boat had been obtained. A front page picture of the vessel in the *Vancouver Province,* accompanied by a restatement of our objectives, heightened the profile of the campaign. The boat itself served as a rallying point to generate public support. We still had to assemble a crew. There were individuals, from the public and the press, who had indicated their desire to get involved directly in the campaign. Aside from Captain Cormack, the Engineer, and myself, there were 9 places to be filled.

Having learned a lesson from the voyage of the *Golden Rule,* the Quaker protest vessel of the 1950s, we believed that extensive media involvement would be crucial to the success of our campaign. The *Golden Rule* had had no media people onboard; this resulted in very little reporting of their action, and what did get reported, were the words of the authorities, who had arrested the crew and had the ship taken in tow. We wanted to be in full control of what the public heard. It also occurred to us that full-time, direct contact with the outside world might also serve as a deterrent should the U.S. think to sink the boat on the high sea.

We bought, or leased, state-of-the-art communication and navigation equipment and decided that four spaces should be reserved for the media: two print journalists, one radio commentator, and one photographer. These four would fulfill the onboard function of reporting what transpired.

Irving then sent an open letter to the newspapers requesting volunteers for the voyage. Robert Hunter, a *Vancouver Sun* columnist applied, as did Ben Metcalfe, a CBC commentator, and Bob Cummings, a reporter from the alternative press, the *Georgia Straight*. Robert Keziere, a professional still photographer, rounded out the media component.

The balance of the ship's company was comprised of Lyle Thurston, a physician, Terry Simmons, a cultural geographer and Sierra Club rep, Bill Darnell, Sierra Club and Greenpeace name inventor, Patrick Moore, ecologist/physicist, and Richard Fineberg, a free-lance journalist with high level U.S. press connections—a last minute addition to the crew.

Regular weekly meetings were usually held at one or other of our homes, but as time went on, the number attending grew so large, meetings had to be scheduled at the Fireside Room of the Unitarian Church. We continued our preparations for our September 15th sailing date to Amchitka.

In 1970, President Richard Nixon signed into law the Environmental Protection Act. This led to the formation of the Environmental Protection Agency, which had the mandate of monitoring the environmental impacts of any activity which involved U.S. government funds or territory. The Act called for full disclosure of plans, the impact on the environment, descriptions of suggested mitigation measures, and, most importantly, the consequences if proposed activity was not permitted to go forward.

Imagine the confusion and outrage of the nuclear testing proponents. The Atomic Energy Commission would now be required to make available, heretofore, secret plans to the general public for critical analysis and comment. Hearings were scheduled in Juneau, the capital of Alaska, and in Anchorage, where the 1964 earthquake in the Aleutians wreaked its greatest damage to life and property. Pat Moore and I attended both these hearings.

Jeremy Stone, Executive Director of the Union of Concerned Scientists, was one of the most effective, and knowledgeable, critics. His testimony, and that of scores of experts—meteorologists, geologists, oceanographers—warned of the possible consequences of the planned Cannikin 5-megaton test. It was here, at these hearings, that test proponents admitted that hundreds of endangered sea otters had been washed up on the Amchitka shore line a few weeks after the Milrow explosion. The shock wave that surged through the waters impacted on the hearing organs of the otters, deafening them. No longer able to hear, the otters, disoriented, simply died of starvation. A 5-megaton explosion would certainly threaten destruction to the remaining population.

It was clear to us that our fears were not nearly as severe as what the reality could be, yet, the scientists from the Department of Energy continued to proclaim the safety of the tests. As Pat Moore later commented to the press: "If they think it's so safe, then why don't they test the bomb in Kansas."

We still had to make the *Phyllis Cormack* shipshape. There were eleven bunks; the twelfth was upstairs in the wheelhouse and served as the Captain's quarters. The bunk room adjoined a combined galley/eating area. There was one small wash basin, no shower facilities, and the only toilet was outside—a privy. These accommodations were not only primitive, they were covered with the grime of years.

A cursory examination of the engine room revealed much the same story. The encrusted ancient Atlas diesel engine evidently was not securely fastened to the main structural members of the boat. It was shored in place with sections of wood 2x4s to the adjoining bulkhead. The scuppers were filled with dirty, oil soaked water.

The one life boat, sitting on deck, was also full of water. The skipper said this was the only way the lapstrake hull was sure to be leakproof. The only mitigating factor was the basic soundness of the *Phyllis Cormack*'s hull. It was stout and made from gumwood, a tried and tested, rugged and rot resistant, shipbuilding material.

The *Phyllis Cormack* had originally been used for halibut packing. Of its 84-foot length, more than half of the below deck had contained ice used to keep the accumulated halibut catch from smaller fish-boats fresh; upon its return to the home base, the ice-packed halibut would be sold to fish buyers. We put the ice hold to a far different use.

Not knowing the exact amount of time that we were prepared to commit to the voyage proved to be a sticking point; crew members had jobs and family responsibilities to consider. We created an operational window of six weeks duration. Over that time we would always be at sea. We would have to carry enough fuel and food onboard. We assumed that no port of call, within the Aleutian chain of islands, would allow us to refuel, or re-provision, the boat.

The unmodified *Phyllis Cormack* could remain at sea for about two weeks without refueling. So we loaded the hold with twenty-five, 250-gallon household oil tanks. Each was rigged so that it was a simple matter to pump them into the engine's regular diesel bunkers. The most difficult task was tying the tanks down to prevent shifting in the rough seas. Taking our lead from the propped up diesel engine, we propped, chocked, and otherwise secured the tanks so that even in the fiercest weather they would not break loose from their moorings.

Since Chunky Woodward, then President of Woodward's Department Store chain, offered to stock us with six weeks rations—at cost—Marie made sure no one would suffer from lack of quality or quantity.

The Crew of the *Phyllis Cormack* (*Greenpeace*)

By September of 1971, the crew of the *Greenpeace* had been assembled.

Dave Birmingham, aged 55, was a marine engineer who had served in the Canadian Merchant Marine during WWII, and survived the sinking of two freighters in the North Atlantic. His wife, Deeno, was a charter member of the B.C. Voice of Women, and for many years the editor of the their newsletter. The Birmingham family were activist anti-nuclear protesters. Dave's job was to keep the mechanical equipment operating.

Myself, Jim Bohlen, aged 45, a mechanical engineer, was employed as a Research Scientist in the newly created Ministry of the Environment at the Forest Products Laboratory, University of British Columbia. As representative of the DMAWC onboard, I was the purser, navigator, and the campaign coordinator. My wife, Marie, was the provider of food and head of the cleaning crew of the *Greenpeace*. She served on the shore-based DMAWC ongoing protest group. She was a professional nature illustrator.

John Cormack, aged 60, owner and Captain of the *Phyllis Cormack*, had full control of the vessel, and worked with me in planning the course direction, duration, and functions of the action. His wife, Phyllis, was a schoolteacher in Richmond, B.C.

Bob Cummings, aged 30, was a journalist and music critic for the *Georgia Strait*, Vancouver's underground newspaper. He was on assignment from his paper to report on the goings on aboard the *Greenpeace*. Bob was unmarried.

Bill Darnell, aged 25, was an organizer for the Company of Young Canadians (CYC), a Federal Government initiative aimed at building the social consciousness of Canada's young adults, and a member of the Sierra Club. Bill functioned as cook. His wife Elaine was a member of the DMAWC onshore protest group and a schoolteacher.

Richard Fineberg, aged 30, was a last minute replacement for Lou Hogan, who would have been the only woman on the voyage. The Captain objected to this on the grounds that women brought bad luck. Richard was a political science Ph.D., and represented the U.S. press. He was unmarried.

Bob Hunter, aged 30, was a columnist with the *Vancouver Sun*, assigned by his paper, to cover the Amchitka voyage. He was one of the first to report the Milrow test, and was present at the Peace Arch border blockade. His wife, Zoe, was from the UK and marched to Aldermaston, a nuclear weapons manufacturing plant. The campaign for Nuclear Disarmament, headed by philosopher Bertrand Russell, organized this March.

Bob Keziere, aged 30, was a graduate chemist and photographer for the Amchitka voyage. He wrote the technical background paper (reprinted here as the Appendix) for the DMAWC. He was unmarried.

Ben Metcalfe, aged 50, was current events commentator on CBC radio and one of the first investigative reporters. His prying into organized crime resulted in his being savagely beaten and left for dead in a ditch alongside a Vancouver road. He organized and paid, out of his own pocket, for a billboard display that read, "Ecology, the last Fad." Ben was to link to radio and wire services, with the aim of making the Greenpeace voyage a household topic around the world. His wife Dorothy turned the Metcalfe house into an on-shore communications center from which she relayed messages from the *Greenpeace* to the world media.

Pat Moore, aged 25, was a graduate student at UBC, studying ecology. He was drawn to Greenpeace as an expression of his anger against the Government allowing the gross pulp mill pollution of Nuratosis Inlet on northern Vancouver Island. He was to work with Leonard Walker, a former assistant to the head of the Swedish Atomic Energy Authority, to test for the presence of radiation in the nuclear test area.

Terry Simmons, aged 25, was a teaching assistant at Simon Fraser University, co-founder of the Sierra Club of B.C., and Council representative to the parent U.S. Sierra Club. He was a cultural geographer with a particular interest in the native populations of the Aleutian Islands and was to help on campaign objectives. He was unmarried.

Lyle Thurston, M.D., aged 35, was a medical general practitioner in private practice and the ship's physician. Myron was his partner.

Ready to Sail

Several days before we were due to sail, John Cormack received a letter rescinding the Federal Government guarantee of the *Phyllis Cormack's* insurance policy. When Bob Hunter heard about this outrageous political manoeuver, he wrote a blistering column in the *Vancouver Sun*, denouncing the act as cowardly, un-Canadian, and more. Ben Metcalfe recorded this calumny on an audio-tape, which was widely broadcasted, and Bob Cummings wrote an incensed column for the *Georgia Straight*. These critically worded diatribes evidently embarrassed the Minister; he quickly reinstated the insurance, with the bureaucratic caveat that the *Phyllis Cormack* be seen as "going fishing." Several of us grabbed halibut floats and various other fishing gear, and displayed them on deck.

The Federal Fisheries were a part of the Ministry of the Environment in the Trudeau Government. The Minister of the Environment was Jack Davis, MP from West Vancouver. Davis' portfolio also included the Canadian Forest Service which had management jurisdiction over the Forest Products Laboratory where I was employed. The Director of the FPL was informed that I should be disciplined for participating in the Amchitka protest. And if I persisted, I was to be fired. The Director, to his everlasting credit, told the powers that be that this laboratory was his turf, and if anyone was going to be disciplined, he would be the judge.

The Director did, however, put a letter in my dossier which strongly suggested that I was not to mention my connection with the Forest Products Laboratory in public statements. I had no problem with this constraint.

Finally, We Sail

September 15, 1971, was a beautiful, warm, sun-filled west coast late summer day. We set a course for the fueling dock in Coal Harbour, adjacent to Dead Man's Island where the *Greenpeace's* diesel tanks and the auxiliary fuel tanks would be pumped full. On the way from False Creek around Stanley Park, I was at the steering wheel, Captain Cormack alongside. When I asked him where I should steer for, he replied, somewhat contemptuously, "straight ahead." John clearly was not impressed with our qualifications as seafarers. He referred to us as 33-pounders (a salty term, the equivalent of 'greenhorn').

Our initial press release advised that the *Greenpeace* would be at the Coal Harbour fuel dock at a certain time. It was there that the press could film the boat and interview the crew. When we arrived at the dock no press were in sight, so we decided to circle the dock a few times, until the press had gathered—better late than never. Cormack was very unhappy about that event; he hadn't been consulted beforehand. I agreed with him, but noted that it was very important that our send-off be properly recorded, and that we, at this early stage in the voyage, had to do, what we had to do, in order to accommodate the press.

While the boat was loading, several members of the crew got tanked at the nearest watering hole, missing the 2:00p.m. take-off from the National Harbours Board Fishing Terminal False Creek mooring spot. They showed up at the Gulf fuel dock in Coal Harbour. Others spent teary moments with their respective loved ones. Marie told me later, she was prepared never to see me alive again, her concern having been due to a phone call I had received at home the night before we were to sail.

The caller said he was a fisherman who had known John Cormack for many years and agreed that he was a competent captain. The problem, he went on to say, was the *Phyllis Cormack*: the boat had sunk on two previous occasions and he doubted whether it would get as far as Prince Rupert. I couldn't bring myself to tell the rest of the crew: some were already having last minute doubts, and for all I knew, the caller's story may very well have been malicious nonsense. Captain Cormack was unaware of any previous sinking, though, he did admit he didn't know the full history of the ship.

Great way to start a journey: the Captain had no faith in the crew, the crew had no faith in the boat. If we were to have a successful campaign, I had my work cut out for me.

The afternoon sun was low in the sky as we headed off for Amchitka, seas were calm. We quietly thought our own thoughts as we began the process of adjusting to a different environment. We navigated north-northwest into the Georgia Strait. Our first scheduled stop was to be Prince Rupert where a local group of Greenpeace people, and the general public, were going to greet us, and wish us a *bon voyage.*

There was a planned sail-by at Comox and Campbell River, but at daybreak on September 16th, we had a favorable tide direction in Discovery Passage; the tide ripped through the narrow gap at 9 knots. Since this was about the top speed of the *Greenpeace,* prudence dictated that we abandon the Campbell River sail by, for to do so would have delayed our arrival at Prince Rupert.

Soon after negotiating Discovery Passage, into Johnstone Strait, a float plane landed next to the boat. We were initially apprehensive, thinking we were about to get busted, but it turned out to be a photo crew from the National Film Board. After an hour or so of filming and doing interviews, the NFB crew packed up. Barry Howell, the producer, told me he hadn't been able to get authorization to go any further, but would leave a camera and film with Ben Metcalfe. During the afternoon of that same day, we were closely overflown by a Department of Transport helicopter.

As we headed northwest in Johnstone Strait towards the Inside Passage, we motored past the village of Alert Bay, on Malcolm Island. It was nearly sundown. There was a small crowd of people cheering and waving to us. We knew that Alert Bay was mainly populated by the Kwagiulth people, and were encouraged that news of our voyage had evoked such interest. A native, in an outboard, came alongside and invited us to stop for a moment at the town's fish pier. On arrival, we were greeted by Daisy Sewid, daughter of the Chief. The native people gave us a gift of freshly caught salmon, and invited us to stop again on our return. They planned to dedicate the new Kwagiulth longhouse, and to erect a totem pole in celebration.

Progressing northward through the Queen Charlotte Strait, we entered the Inside Passage at Smith Sound. We cruised by Namu, a town in obvious decline, which, according to Captain Cormack, had thrived when the fishing resource was sufficient to support a large fish cannery. It was shortly after passing Namu, that the *Greenpeace* developed some kind of engine trouble. Abruptly, Captain Cormack steered for Klemtu, another native village suffering from a declining fishery. While the necessary repairs were being made, we took stock of our first days at sea.

We were scheduled to stop at Prince Rupert where anti-nuclear protesters had organized receptions, and where we had considered laying over until a firm date for the Cannikin blast was announced, but the strong possibility that Federal Drug Enforcement officers might board to search for illegal drugs, existed. If they were successful, they could impound the boat, thereby preventing us from going any further. The strong possibility that there may, indeed, be a stash of illegal drugs onboard, also existed.

Captain Cormack said that if there *were* drugs onboard, there were many places where they could be hidden. I was unwilling to take any chances on being stopped, especially in view of the sneaky attempt by Jack Davis to take away the boat's insurance. After a great deal of thought and discussion, and with the support of the rest of the crew, I made the decision to abort our Prince Rupert visit, and instead head out to the North Pacific Ocean towards Amchitka.

Assessing the Crew

The plan to call in at Prince Rupert had been questionable from the start; we constantly worried about being busted. From a logistical aspect, we had no firm date as to when the bomb test was going to occur. If Prince Rupert had been closer to Amchitka, it would have made more sense to tuck in there, but Prince Rupert put us only 600 miles closer to the bomb.

The distance from Vancouver to Amchitka is 2400 miles. This would leave 1800 miles between Prince Rupert and Amchitka. Considering that the *Greenpeace* was capable of cruising at about 9 or 10 knots, this meant, at the very least, 150 hours to sail from Prince Rupert to Amchitka. Since only a 48-hour notice to mariners is required before detonating the bomb, there was no way we would be there in time if we hung around Prince Rupert. We had no alternative but to press on.

At Butedale, 150 miles south of Prince Rupert, we topped up the fuel and water tanks. Butedale was another abandoned village, though an interesting one. Owned outright by a private corporation, it was for sale, at $100,000. There were about 50 well-built houses, served by a regularly maintained hydro-electric facility which provided light and heat for the homes and the fish plant.

During those first few quiet nights, I had the opportunity to reflect upon the diverse group of people who made up the crew: Terry Simmons and Bill Darnell, Sierra Club associates; Bob Hunter, Ben Metcalfe, and Bob Cummings, media; Dave Birmingham, marine engineer; Doc Thurston, Richard Fineberg, Bob Keziere, Pat Moore, and, of course, myself. Ranging in age from 35 to 60, united for one purpose: to confront the bomb.

The most difficult task was to determine the functional relationship between the media personnel and the rest of the crew. Should they be considered passengers or members of the crew? Should they be a part of the decision making process, or were they simply to go along with whatever was decided?

In searching for previous examples where media personnel witnessed the action, I recalled that the front line war correspondents who reported directly from the field were afforded no say in the conduct of the campaign. They took their chances and many lost their lives or were wounded.

The Greenpeace action directly involved twelve men. Four of them were media representatives. They were selected on the basis of their technical skills, not on their commitment to the cause. However, all of them were onboard for campaign related reasons as well as performing their media duties. They also made up one-third of those onboard.

Appreciating the fact that there was some risk to each and every crew member, I mulled over the problem of how we should arrive at decisions. Would we vote on each decision, and if so, who was eligible to vote? Who was not? And if not, what decision-making process should be involved?

But when we got right down to it, the reality of the situation simplified it: John Cormack owned the boat. The terms of his charter spelled out the actions of the campaign would not involve impoundment of the *Greenpeace*. I, as the onboard representative of the charterer, the Don't Make a Wave Committee, had to assume the authority of what amounted to tactical command of the campaign.

Once I accepted, however reluctantly, it was possible to include everybody in the process of strategic decision making, with the proviso that Captain Cormack had veto power, should any decision by the group contradict the terms of his charter, and, that the DMAWC, through me, also had a veto should decisions involve the expenditure of resources that the Committee could not afford.

Media Representation Onboard the *Greenpeace*

Bob Keziere was the still photographer; he was given the freedom to photograph whomever, doing whatever. Bob Hunter was in the employ of the *Vancouver Sun*; his job was to write a daily column for his newspaper. Ben Metcalfe was onboard as a free-lance TV and radio correspondent; his job was to maintain 24-hour a day contact with the regional, national, and global press. (Logistically, he would send messages *via* single sideband radio to his Vancouver based wife, Dorothy, who would then put these communiques onto the various wire services.) Bob Cummings was an employee of the *Georgia Straight*; and Richard Fineberg wrote extensively from a U.S. citizen's perspective.

Media output was never censored, nor peer reviewed; they were reliable and professional, and did their jobs well.

The Crossing

With an unlikely crew, a questionably serviceable boat, and no firm date for the Cannikin blast, we headed across the North Pacific, motoring past Langara Island on the flat calm of the Dixon Entrance waters off the Queen Charlottes, waved good-bye to this *most* western land of Canada, and headed out towards Dutch Harbor in the Aleutian chain. Although Dutch Harbor was more than a 48-hour sail to Amchitka, there we would be able to secure supplies: fuel, water, food. There was, however, one catch: we needed to have the approval of the U.S. Coast Guard to call in at Dutch Harbour.

On the morning of September 18th, we felt a noticeable roll of the boat. Since leaving Vancouver, we had sailed the calm waters of the Inside Passage. Today, we would find out who among us had our sea legs. Dr. Thurston was prepared to dole out Gravol to offset any seasickness.

By sunset, the roll increased dramatically: the waves had reached a height of 14 feet! They broke sharply over the stern making a trip to the toilet a struggle: the only access was from the stern level, and if not carefully timed, a dash to the toilet meant a cold soaking. Inside the ship, the pitching and rolling caused everything that wasn't firmly lashed down to fly everywhere. Captain Cormack gave us a quick lesson in what 'shipshape' meant.

In my Navy days I had occasion to operate the radio directed navigation system called Loran (the acronym standing for Long Range Navigation). There were published charts which indicated the location of shore-based Loran master/slave transmitters. By locating any two transmitter locations with a radio direction finder one could triangulate and calculate the position of the boat with great accuracy. It was 25 years since I had learned to use Loran and I was a bit tentative about the mechanics of setting a great circle route for Dutch Harbor.

After plotting the course several times in the span of eight hours or so, I checked in with the wheel-man to verify the compass heading. Panic ensued. Although the compass indicated that the boat was pointed right on course, my Loran fixes indicated that the boat was going around in circles.

I told the captain. He went up to the wheelhouse, took a cursory look. What he saw only confirmed, in his mind, our incompetence. Someone had placed their tape recorder on top of the magnetic compass and had turned it on. The magnetic field around the compass was being affected by the electromagnetic impressions of the tape recorder, and in turn, affected the direction indicated by the compass dial. Since the tape recorder was only on intermittently, the compass righted itself when the recorder was turned off, and consequently there were a host of compass readings that had absolutely no relevance to where we were actually headed.

After straightening out that navigational problem, we experienced no further incidents relative to navigating. The Loran system consistently indicated that we were headed on a direct great circle course towards Dutch Harbor.

The harmony of our journey was again broken on September 23rd, when it was announced by the U.S. Atomic Energy Commission that there would be a delay in the date of the test blast. It was tentatively rescheduled for October 20th. We also found out early the next day, September 24th, that the U.S. Coast Guard cutter *Balsam* had been tailing us. We learned about this from Vancouver where the permission to call in at Dutch Harbor, made by Dorothy Metcalfe, had, that day, been denied.

We now pretty much knew what the overflights by the U.S. Air Force were all about. We were at last being taken seriously as potential interferers in the plans of U.S. authorities to explode the Cannikin nuclear bomb. They were now trying to manipulate *us*. They had allowed us to get to the mid-crossing point between Prince Rupert and Dutch Harbor before they announced the delay of the test. They probably hoped our range was limited to a single crossing of the North Pacific, and that after denying us access to an Alaskan port where we could refuel and resupply, a lack of fuel would force us to return to a Canadian port.

If correct, we would have had only one alternative: return to Prince Rupert. But the U.S. operatives did not know we had jammed the hold of the *Greenpeace* with fuel-filled auxiliary tanks that would permit us to remain at sea for six weeks—until October 27th.

What amounted to a game of chess was about to be played out between the most powerful nation in the world and a band of twelve volunteers. Each of us had been prepared to devote six weeks to the Amchitka campaign. Although the new date for the test was set for October 20, it still fell within our time commitment, but only just. The biggest problem we now faced was what to do between now, September 23rd, and October 20th—almost one month! We hadn't prepared for this.

Between a Rock and a Hard Place

Our protest was quickly attracting support. A nationwide movement against nuclear testing was beginning to grow in intensity. Support for our action was building and contributions began to flow into the Don't Make a Wave Committee. As well, in the United States, the Cannikin test was being brought to the Supreme Court for a decision. Senator Gravel of Alaska spoke out in opposition. Biologists were voicing their concern about the possibility of multiple sea otter deaths. We had become the leading edge of a massive opposition to nuclear testing. We had to come up with something for the intervening month that would keep public attention focused. And, too, we needed to keep our own adrenalin flowing. I knew from my experience as a sailor in the U.S. Navy how debilitating idleness could be. Many times I had been awakened at 4:00a.m. and told to pack my gear for this or that activity. And then sat on my pack for hours, just waiting for the action to happen, bored and discouraged.

We knew we could not turn back and wait; we would certainly lose media interest, public interest, and possibly the interest of some of the crew. Playing out the waiting game by going back home would be a disaster: on that point we were unanimous. But what to do between now and the test date? We reinstated our singular objective: the confrontation of the bomb. As to exactly what course of action that confrontation led to, was open to interpretation.

An obvious one, was to sail up to the 3-mile limit and simply sit there until the bomb went off, or, the test was canceled. Captain Cormack was not happy with this scenario, primarily because of the amount of fuel it would take to run the ship while at anchor for one month without the possibility of re-fueling. Since we had already been denied entry to Dutch Harbor—the closest refueling point—we would have been at the mercy of the elements and/or the generosity of the U.S. Coastguard, either through towing us to Dutch Harbour, or re-fueling us from their tankage.

Another option was to swing past Amchitka and call in at Vladivostok, on the Kamchatka Peninsula, and while there protest the USSR's nuclear testing program, and, if we had sufficient time, to call at Shanghai to protest China's testing of nuclear weapons. The Captain was not enthused by this plan either: chances of having his vessel impounded grew more likely. As well, he feared the unstable weather and the treacherous waters of the North Pacific Ocean and the Bering Sea. The *Greenpeace* was a chartered boat; we could not insist that the owner place it at risk.

A third possibility was to sail up to the 3-mile limit right now, launch a small boat, with a few of the crew, land on Amchitka as close as possible to the test site, then, hike to the site and perform a sit-in as close to the detonation point as possible. We would stay there to 'witness' the bomb blast, or until we were arrested.

Here was a plan! But how were we to do it? The only small boat available was a lapstrake hulled, leaky, wooden, oar-propelled auxiliary craft that had little chance of going the distance. And, we did not know exactly where the bomb was to be detonated. We had no 'mole' in the AEC to supply us with that information. We did decide, however, to ask the DMAWC, in Vancouver, to look for wet suits, ASAP. (Years later, high speed engine driven small rubber boats named Zodiacs by their French inventors, became available. Greenpeace would be the first to use them in water-based campaigns. The speed, maneuverability, and the effectiveness of Zodiac craft soon shaped the public image of Greenpeace as a can-do effective protector of the natural environment.)

We were running out of options, but had come too far to simply return home. I made one final appeal to Captain Cormack. By now, he must have felt some pity for the plight of his 33-pounders, for after a few moments of thought, he began to speak of an island where Canadian halibut fishermen often took shelter in foul weather, or when they had mechanical problems. By putting in to an Aleutian Island safe harbor we could maintain the interest of the public, for it would be seen as having, essentially, reached our objective.

Captain Cormack opted for Akutan Island: a protected harbor, few mountains, and a town-site of about 800 native Aleuts. There, a float plane delivered the mail and supplies twice a week. Since we would be at anchor in calm waters, we would not have to consume any fuel to maintain our vigil. As well, our radio contact with the outside world would not be blocked from the many high mountains which constituted much of the Aleutian Island chain.

Unknown to us, we were under constant surveillance by the Coast Guard as we headed for Akutan Harbor. Also, at the time, we had found it curious that our radio broadcasts had not been jammed by the U.S. authorities. Later we learned our choice of single sideband transmission frequencies was the major radio communication method and frequency of the North Pacific fishing fleet. Jamming of that station might have jeopardized the safety of vessels needing assistance.

Cormack radioed the Coast Guard in Anchorage, Alaska, that his ship was experiencing mechanical difficulties, and consequently, he was putting in at Akutan. Hearing no 'negatives,' we sailed for Akutan, arriving there on September 26th.

We had achieved the limited objective of reaching the Aleutian Chain, and were tucked into a safe harbour with sufficient fuel to cover the remaining 900 miles in four days, bear witness to the explosion, and return to Vancouver. In the meantime, we could spend some time ashore, learn about the native people, and explore this remarkable Akutan Island.

Our one-week stay at Akutan was, at once, both wonderful and terrible. While exploring the shoreline we came upon a rusting mess of iron plate and pipe that turned out to be an abandoned whale processing factory. These stations existed in almost every island of the Aleutians and were active prior to the time of the factory whaling ship. After catching a number of whales, the whaling vessels of old would put in to Akutan, or some similar place, and maneuver the dead whale carcasses where they were winched up from the water's edge into the whale processing facility. They were cut up, the blubber boiled and the whale oil squeezed out. What remained of the carcass was simply discarded on the beach, gleaned by the shore birds, and bleached by the wave action and heavy rains. There they were, enormous rib cages sticking out of the gravely sand, a memorial to the presumption of man who felt he had the right to take the life of these magnificent creatures—to light a few lamps, to feed a few dogs, and to make fertilizer.

Where were the whales now? We had not seen any. The natives confirmed the whales were no longer. Gone also were the sea otters, hunted to extinction for the Russian fur-trade.

With the disappearance of these natural renewable resources, the native Aleuts economy had been destroyed, and their 9,000 years of existence as a culturally vigorous people living in harmony with their environment, seemed to be coming to an end.

We had arrived at Akutan soon after the Alaskan native land claims had been settled. A certain portion of the settlement had been in the form of a cash dividend to each native person, the intention being that the money be re-invested in some alternative income-creating scheme. This had not to occured. Instead, the Akutans were resentful and had largely turned to drink. When we first landed, the natives were openly hostile, although that attitude softened when they learned that we were going up against the United States Government nuclear testing program.

The previously discussed scenario of the *Greenpeace* lying at anchor outside the 3-mile limit of Amchitka while an auxiliary small boat made for shore and then overland to the test site, was never completely abandoned. To test the feasibility of an overland approach to the test site, Bill Darnell and I headed across Akutan Island with a backpack containing some foul weather gear and sufficient food for a one-day hike.

As we hiked, we realized the steep rise and fall of the slopes that led from the shore into the interior. They were covered, in abundance, with long green grasses, wild flowers, and, curiously, a miniaturized community of evergreens: trees that would have grown into giants elsewhere along the Alaskan coast. In the Aleutians, the constant winds whistling across the land made it impossible for the trees to grow any higher than the crown of the surrounding grasses. All in all a wildly beautiful sight.

Unknown to Bill and I was the existence of feral cattle once husbanded by the Russians when they occupied the island in the 1850s. In following a trail that led across to the Bering Sea shoreline, we saw large piles of what could only be animal spoor. But the size! What kind of animal could it be? We were thinking Kodiak grizzly, the largest carnivore next to the Polar bear. We were imagining an encounter on the trail with a thousand pounds of bulk, claws and teeth sharp and long, tearing into our flesh. What a relief, and a pleasant surprise, when, later in the day, we saw the reality of our concern—a full-sized cow, placidly munching the tundra grasses.

On reaching the Bering Sea side of Akutan, we saw that the sand was coal black: lava spill from some ancient volcano. The whole Aleutian chain is volcanic in origin. On some of the islands large volcanic mountains often vent plumes of smoke, giving notice of the devastating potential that lies beneath the surface. It was just this possibility of disaster, triggered by a deep underground nuclear blast, that seismologists testified to at the Cannikin environmental impact hearings in Juneau and Anchorage.

Bill and I saw, too, a proliferation of flotsam and jetsam: glass floats, discarded nets, unending in length, plastic bags, containers, and other garbage tossed overboard from passing ships. We saw partially eaten birds that had been trapped in the netting. Everywhere we looked, human garbage along the shoreline, proof of just how immense the fishing fleets were. The entire ecosystem of the Bering Sea irreparably damaged.

If such was the state of wilderness, the fate of the Planet seemed sealed, and as we sat and ate our cheese sandwiches, we imagined humans roving the oceans, unrestricted by any sense of responsibility towards sustainability, robbing them of every living thing. Bill and I trudged back to base, shocked and dismayed.

For me, this was a highlight of the voyage. To have had the opportunity to explore such a remote part of the world was an experience of a lifetime: both exhilarating, as to the extent and variety in nature, and depressing in the knowledge of what we were doing to this wild magnificence, and to each other. Combined with evidence of the extermination of whales and sea otters, and the impoverished native people, left to wallow in a drunken stupor, I was fully impressed by this catastrophe of ecological destruction. The experience was to change the course of my life.

After Bill and I returned to the *Greenpeace,* the crew discussed, in some detail, how we could find out where on Amchitka the test would take place, and what were the possibilities for a combined sit-in-at-sea and a small boat landing to occupy the detonation site.

Amchitka is about 40 miles long and averages about 3 miles in width. The entire coastline is clifflike and has no satisfactory shelter that might constitute a harbor. An airstrip had been carved out of the tundra and was capable of handling the landings and takeoffs of large cargo planes. We assumed from this that the entire supply operation on Amchitka was by air.

The veil of secrecy surrounding the AEC build up on Amchitka was tightly woven. We exhausted every possibility in the attempt to pinpoint where the bomb site was located. I contacted the DMAWC in Vancouver to make them aware of the need for information. None was forthcoming. We had previously relayed the need for each crew member to have a wet suit; a supplier in Vancouver had been located, and was willing to supply wetsuits at cost. So, body measurements were taken and sent to Irving, who was coordinating events on the Vancouver mainland.

Some crew members worked at repairing the *Greenpeace* row boat, and were able to make it at least serviceable for ferrying us to the Akutan town-site and back to the ship.

On one occasion, several of us climbed the hill behind the village of Akutan. We were in desperate need of a bath. For the first time in weeks the September sun beamed down on the sodden soil. When we stumbled onto a narrow swift flowing stream that descended the hill, we stripped off our clothes and plunged into the water. Frigid, but refreshing. We had no soap, so it was scrape and rinse, which was just as well. We didn't know it then, but we were washing our crud into the drinking water of the residents of Akutan.

Getting Busted

Late on the afternoon of October 1, I was relaxing in my bunk waiting for the call to supper, when I heard the engine start up. I ran out on deck. Dave Birmingham was raising the anchor. Captain Cormack was at the wheel and the *Greenpeace* was headed backwards, further into the Akutan lagoon. Birmingham pointed towards the entrance to the bay. Looming out of the sea in the gathering dark, entering the harbor like some great white apparition was the U.S. Coast Guard ship, *Confidence*.

The *Confidence* anchored at the entrance to the bay, and set down a launch manned by four coast-guardsmen. Standing erect at the bow of the launch, looking somewhat like Washington crossing the Delaware, was Commander Lloyd Hunter, Captain of the *Confidence*. Resplendent in a bright orange wet suit, goggles perched jauntily on his forehead, he hoisted himself aboard the aft deck of the *Greenpeace* as the launch sidled up alongside. Hunter asked to speak with the Captain.

While Commander Hunter spoke with Cormack, the rest of us went out on deck to have a look at the coast-guardsmen who had remained in the launch. No conversation about what we were doing in these waters was necessary; the crew of the *Confidence* knew our mission. Curiously, one of the coast-guardsmen handed up a written statement; it had been signed by 20 or so of the crewmen, and read:

> Due to the situation we are in, the crew of the *Confidence* feel that what you are doing is for the good of all mankind. If our hands were not tied by these military bonds, we would be in the same position that you are in, if it was at all possible. Good luck, we are behind you one hundred per cent.

This remarkable expression of support, coming as it did from our presumed enemy, became the defining experience of the whole campaign: proof we had made the right decision in remaining rather than backtracking. Our presence in the Aleutians had become the focal point for the anti-testing movement.

Our presence in U.S. waters had even managed to capture the minds and hearts of those who were sent to stop us. According to one of the boarding crew, virtually the whole complement of men on the *Confidence* would have signed the telegram had time permitted. Later it came to light that officers who signed the petition were demoted one rank, fined three months without pay, and enlisted men were given a stern reprimand.

According to Commander Hunter, Captain Cormack had not notify the Coast Guard at Anchorage, Alaska, of our arrival in Akutan, within the 24 hours allowed. He was in violation of Section 19 USCG 1435 of U.S. Coast Guard regulations. This violation of U.S. maritime law could result in a fine of $5,000, and/or, impoundment of the vessel. We were now firmly in the grip of the U.S. authorities.

News of the bust gave tremendous impetus to this mainly Canadian initiative. For the first time the U.S. media picked up on the protest and gave it serious and widespread attention. Not only were we pleased, but reporting of the event served also those in the United States who were opposed to the testing. The whole North American anti-war movement was focused on the Amchitka test. The issue went to the U.S. Supreme Court and President Nixon.

Paradoxically, the legal challenge to the Cannikin test had adverse effects with regard to our plan of confronting the bomb. Not willing to set off the Cannikin bomb before the Supreme Court ruled on it, the AEC was obliged to postpone the test until a decision was rendered. Protesters in the U.S. were not mindful of our time schedule limitations, and so there was not any particular effort in the States to campaign for a quick decision. On the other hand, speeding up the court process would also be to the advantage of the AEC. Postponements were costly for them due to mounting expenses incurred in maintaining staff and equipment at the test site.

In assessing the consequences of the bust it appeared that the campaign had accomplished a major objective: we had thrust to the forefront the issue of nuclear testing to the attention of the North American public. The next phase was to attempt to confront the bomb if, and when, permission to detonate it was given by Richard Nixon.

Going Backwards to go Forward

It was in the evening of October 1st, that Captain Cormack spoke of his conversation with Commander Hunter. He had agreed to leave Akutan the next morning; the new destination would be Sand Point, the nearest Customs and Immigration station. Sand Point, located on Popof Island in the Shumagin Island group, was in a direction away from Amchitka. This news hit hard, and after supper that evening, the crew met to re-group.

One thing was crystal clear: John Cormack was not about to risk the impoundment of his boat. His contract with the DMAWC specifically addressed this point. We could no longer expect to confront the bomb directly. At best, we could lie at anchor three miles offshore at some unknown point along the 80 mile coastline of Amchitka Island.

Early on the morning of October 2nd, the *Greenpeace* motored out of Akutan and headed northeast towards the Shumagin Islands. As soon as we cleared the headland of Akutan Bay the boat began to roll from side to side. At the same time, the bow and stern pitched up and down. We were in the throw of the *williwaws*: violent and unpredictable wave motions caused by high velocity winds sweeping from the Bering Sea over treeless terrain and funneled through mountain valleys. These winds were often accompanied by icy blasts from the Arctic regions of the Bering Sea that whip the waves into a frozen foam, coating rigging and superstructure in minutes. Ships have turned turtle from the destabilized effect of ice accumulating only on one side of the boat. The violence of *williwaw* generated seas have actually broken brand new steel hulled fishing vessels in half, sinking them and drowning the crew in cold waters.

Here we were, 33-pounders, in the grip of a North Pacific storm that sent more than one of us crawling toward bunks. The operation of the *Greenpeace* fell to the few standing.

With the storm approaching full intensity, we steered for the shelter of the Shumagin Islands, arriving there on the evening of October 2nd, and dropped anchor in the protected waters. Tired, and disappointed, we fell into our bunks.

Decisions, Decisions

On the morning of October 3rd, with the storm over, we headed for the customs port, Sand Point. We had no idea what to expect upon arrival. Would we be welcomed, or arrested? We didn't even know if our radio could reach Vancouver. We docked alongside the King Crab processing plant, shut down the main engine, and secured the boat. Captain Cormack got his papers together, including the citation from the *Confidence*'s Commander, and he and I walked the quarter mile to the Harbormaster's office and Customs and Immigration.

We were treated politely, but coolly, by the government personnel. After a superficial examination of Cormack's paperwork, we cleared Customs, but not before the Immigration officer read us the riot act: We had committed a serious infraction of the immigration laws of the United States of America by going ashore at Akutan, especially the Canadian citizens who could be charged with illegally entering the United States. There was no indication given as to whether or not individuals *would* be prosecuted. We were told to expect a $500 fine for each infraction. As to the *Greenpeace*, in view of Captain Cormack having followed Coast Guard orders, there would be no impoundment. The *Greenpeace* was free to leave Sand Point.

On the way to the Harbormaster's office I had noticed a public telephone booth at the far end of the dock. Ben Metcalfe was already there beaming messages back to his wife Dorothy in Vancouver. When he was through, I phoned Irving Stowe. What he told me warmed my heart: Irving said in a few days there was to be a public demonstration against Cannikin in every major city in Canada. Pierre Burton, the noted Canadian historian and writer, was conducting a cross-Canada call-in radio program to speak out against Cannikin, and to solicit funds for the DMAW cause.

Then, Irving spoke excitedly of looking for another, faster, boat for charter. He said we had $25,000 in the bank: all expenses to date, paid. The second boat could be used as backup; it could be put into service if the bomb blast were further delayed. But I had my doubts. Amchitka was 2400 miles from Vancouver, and again, with the 48-hour notice, the vessel would have to be able to cover 1200 miles a day, at 50 miles per hour. No oceangoing vessel that I knew of was capable of maintaining that speed for 48 hours.

Until the U.S. Supreme Court ruling came down, we had to assume that the date of the Cannikin test was still October 20th. Meanwhile, public pressure was building across Canada and the U.S. On October 6th, 10,000 students from Vancouver public schools made their way to the U.S. consulate in downtown Vancouver—a display of opposition to the testing of nuclear weapons exceeded only by the anti-nuclear demonstrations of the mid-60s at Aldermaston, UK.

The DMAWC was ecstatic about the campaign; all of Canada seemed united in support. Many were of the opinion we had achieved a clear victory and should return home and savor our accomplishments. That many did not include the crew; we were not content to travel backwards. The bomb had not yet been set off, and we still had use of the *Greenpeace* for three more weeks.

Sand Point was 900 miles from Amchitka. Given the 48-hour notice, and our top cruising speed of 8 knots in a calm sea, it would take about 110 hours to reach Amchitka, non-stop, from Sand Point. But, if we left Sand Point five days before the October 20th test date, arriving at Amchitka on the 19th, we could anchor just outside the 3-mile limit and bear witness. We would prepare for an October 15th departure.

Daily, we checked with Aleutian Airlines for news of the shipment of wet suits from Vancouver—to no avail. More than likely they lay in the corner of some U.S. Customs warehouse, mislaid (intentionally).

Then, Paul Cote and Irving Stowe received word the test had been delayed to "some time in early November." The precise date would be announced by the White House. It seemed to us that the U.S. had also figured out our plan of action and set the test forward in another attempt to keep us from confronting the bomb. Back home, the DMAWC claimed a 'victory' in that our presence within striking distance of the bomb site was causing the U.S. to continue delaying the test date.

With the test postponed again, and not having the slightest idea as to when it would be given the final go-ahead, if ever, we didn't know what to do next. I called the DMAWC in Vancouver and, in the course of the conversation, learned that plans were going forward to secure the second strike boat, to be known as the *Greenpeace Too*.

On the night of October 12th, the crew met again. We had stuck together these long weeks; we had faced disappointments and delays. As one, we had refused to give up, but our courses of action were narrowing. We felt we had two choices: one, to sail into the area, as near as possible to the test site and remain until we ran out of fuel, water or food, or, until the charter with Cormack terminated on October 31st. The other choice was to return home, making ports of call on the way to as many Alaskan and Canadian cities as possible, conducting open ship visitations and discussions, pointing out the dangers of conducting the Cannikin nuclear blast. The port visits could be a test of public opinion, helpful to the DMAWC in assessing the effectiveness of our political strategies.

We needed to achieve consensus, but it was not forthcoming. Darnell, Fineberg, Hunter, and Simmons were insistent that the *Greenpeace* go forward to Amchitka. "Retreating" would be seen as a "defeat." The rest of the crew, with the exception of John Cormack, who stood aside, elected to backtrack and do the publicity oriented ports of call alternative. After hours of wrangling, we took the decision to go back.

Heroes

After breakfast, on October 13th, we set sail for Kodiak, Alaska, our first port of call on the long journey back to Vancouver. The *Greenpeace* set out along the populated southern rim of the Alaska Peninsula, and the mainland of western Canada, intending to visit every community along the coast, weather and time permitting.

The trip from Sand Point to Kodiak was uneventful; the mood onboard despondent. As we entered the harbor at Kodiak, Alaska, and with a mile to go to dockside, a launch positioned itself to come alongside the *Greenpeace*. Again, we were apprehensive, but as the launch neared, the people in the boat stood, waving and shouting their welcomes. Hundreds more well wishers, with banners and placards, welcomed us from land: all arranged by the local anti-Vietnam war group, and supported by the cast of sailors who had been censured for supporting our Amchitka campaign.

We had been taken up as a symbol of protest, not only to the opposition of the Cannikin tests, but to the anti-war movement as well. Our arrival, in Kodiak, had coincided with the military bombing of targets in Cambodia; this escalation was the final straw. And too, still remembered was the earthquake of 1964; Kodiak bore the brunt of that event. Large sections of the City's waterfront had been destroyed, and even now, seven years later, still evident. As well, most Alaskans felt alienated from the lower forty-eight. Since its purchase from the Russian Government in the 1860s by William Seward, U.S. Secretary of State, it had been often referred to as Seward's Folly. Then, Alaska fast became the resource capital of the U.S.: a huge fishery, seemingly unlimited timber, and a wealth of wild animals. And now, oil had been discovered on the North Slope and great pressure was coming to bear upon the Alaskan State Government to approve a massive, and potentially destructive, project.

We were speechless at the enthusiasm with which the people of Kodiak greeted us. First, a celebratory march the length of the town's main street, then a festive dinner in our honor. Two days later, still buoyed by the exuberance of our reception, we sailed out of Kodiak: renewed, rejuvenated, and of the belief that what we had done, and were still doing, was making a real difference.

The weather in the North Pacific suddenly turned treacherous. Captain Cormack insisted we head straight east, across the Gulf of

Alaska, to the shelter of the Inside Passage, without delay. Then, just as suddenly, a fire broke out in the engine room. No sooner did Captain Cormack and Dave Birmingham successfully extinguished it, with rags and their bare hands, when the reverse gear jammed. This alone would have made landing at a dock, even in good weather, something of a miracle. We began to wonder if our good luck was running out.

The shortest route to the Inside Passage was to head due east for Cape Spencer. The nearest port to Cape Spencer was Juneau, the capital of Alaska. Juneau's population, in 1990, was 27,000; in 1971, it was closer to 20,000. Pat Moore and I had been to Juneau as one of the stops on the series of AEC hearings concerning the environmental impact of Cannikin. We were fairly certain of getting a good reception there.

The distance from Kodiak to Juneau was about 500 miles. At an optimistic cruising speed of 8 knots, the *Greenpeace* would need about two and a half days, in calm waters; if the weather turned nasty, a week.

One day out of Kodiak, a fierce storm struck. It raged for three days; 20- to 40-foot waves smashed down on the decks and battered the weathered hull. Rather than steer straight for Cape Spencer, we had to go with the weather, or more accurately, at right angles to the weather, to survive. We had to avoid the troughs between waves, by cutting across them.

John Cormack and I were the only members of the crew that had any extensive experience at sea, and while John bore the brunt of navigating us through the storm, I served as relief when he needed to eat or sleep.

During one of my shifts, while struggling with the wheel to keep a heading into the waves, I felt a shudder that vibrated through the whole boat. A huge wave had literally submerged the fore end. Its 30-foot height struck with full force against the wheel house. Cormack was immediately at my side, grabbing the wheel, helping hold the bow into the waves. "A quare one," he breathed. Later, I learned that when a "quare one" hits, it is usually bye-bye for the boat. It strikes a vessel broadside, without warning; many a fishing boat have been flipped over, sunk, and lost.

As navigator, I turned on the Loran receiver to get a fix on our position. In our desperate attempt to stay headed into the wind, we hadn't paid much attention to the course. I found that instead of going forward towards Cape Spencer, we had actually gone backwards during the last eight hours: the *Greenpeace* had not been able to overcome the counter-thrust of the waves.

Eventually, the storm abated, and, once more, we set a direct course for Cape Spencer. Two days later, on October 20th, we cleared the lighthouse at Cape Spencer, thankful. We had made it to the Inside Passage in one piece, and headed directly for a docking spot in Juneau.

The reception in Juneau was similar to Kodiak. After some confusion as to where we were to dock, and some problems involved with the parking process due to our lack of a reverse gear, the entire crew left the *Greenpeace.* In the company of a few remaining supporters who braved the cold rain and our clumsy docking procedure we were escorted to the Dreamland, a pub-cum-restaurant. For the first time in many weeks I felt relief from the stress of the campaign, the welfare of the crew, and the terms of the charter with Captain Cormack. I let go in Juneau, drinking a few beers and dancing (I am told) for hours.

It was October 21st when we left Juneau and headed south in the calm waters of the Inside Passage. We stopped at Petersburg, which had been the capital of Alaska when it was owned by Russia. Orthodox onion domes of the many churches dotted the skyline. From there, we went to Ketchikan, a fishing town of about 7,000 people, where I listened to a gathering of fishermen express their fear about the long term effects of contamination to the fish population that the Cannikin tests would surely cause.

By October 22nd, we were crossing the U.S./Canada border at the Dixon Entrance. Back in our home country, at last. The people at Prince Rupert radioed us that a welcome had been arranged; hundreds of people in that city wanted to host our visit. We wondered if our Canadian supporters would welcome us with the same degree of enthusiasm as we experienced in Kodiak and Juneau. They did: Fisherman's Hall, in downtown Prince Rupert, was filled to capacity.

We spent the next day admiring the scenery of the Inside Passage. We anchored at the community of Alert Bay on Cormorant Island in the Strait of Georgia.

On the first day of our voyage in mid-September, we had called in at Alert Bay at the request of Daisy Sewid, daughter of chief of the Kwagiulth Indian Band. The Kwagiulth people, and the Haida, had been the pre-eminent tribes from the Queen Charlotte Islands, and south, along the west coast. As their population declined, the Kwagiulth had settled in Alert Bay. There, they had set up a successful fishing industry; hundreds of Kwagiulth-owned fish boats plied the waters of the west coast of Canada. They would bring their catch to the large community-owned processing plant run by the Sewid family. At the time of the Cannikin protest, their cultural heritage was facing a rebirth, and once more splendid totem poles were being carved in celebration. For these reasons, and others, the Kwagiulth were unanimous in their support of our voyage.

As we motored into Alert Bay Harbor, dozens of small craft set out from shore to escort us to dockside. In the village, we were honored by a special ceremony held at the Kwagiulth's new longhouse, and, by an invitation to participate in their tribal (often times, secret) ceremonies.

Young and old, resplendent in costume, performed dance after dance. At one point, an elder sprinkled our bowed heads with feathers, symbolic of 'the flight of the eagle.' Then, we too, were encouraged to join in the ritual dancing. This was our indoctrination into the Kwagiulth Nation as blood brothers of the native people!

The Bomb Goes Off

After weeks of deliberation, hearing many protests from many groups, the U.S. Supreme Court rendered its decision: the Cannikin nuclear weapon test could be conducted. A host of environmental and peace groups formally appealed the decision. If the appeal failed, the test would probably go ahead immediately; the AEC was getting anxious about the delays.

Early on the morning of October 27th, we got the news that another boat, the *Edgewater Fortune*, renamed *Greenpeace Too*, had been chartered, provisioned, crewed, and was ready to sail. The *Greenpeace Too* would leave Vancouver and head directly across the Gulf of Alaska for Amchitka. The boat, a de-commissioned Canadian naval vessel, built in the early-50s, re-christened the *Edgewater Fortune* by its new owner and skipper Hank Johansen, had originally been a minesweeper.

I had some reservations about its stability; it was a minesweeper that was no longer equipped with a system of paravanes. These cigar shaped floats supported the nets which trailed out from the stern of minesweepers trolling to capture floating and submerged mines. The system of paravanes and nets also stabilized the minesweepers. Despite the fact that they were extremely fast (about 25 knots or nearly 36 miles per hour), they were notoriously unstable in heavy seas. And too, the *Edgewater Fortune* was a fuel eater. At 100 gallons per hour, it had just enough fuel storage capacity to make the run to Amchitka, directly across the Pacific, and come right back. By comparison the *Greenpeace* consumed between 7 and 10 gallons of diesel fuel per hour. There was no way the *Edgewater Fortune* could have carried out a sit-in at sea. The closest refueling port was Dutch Harbor. No Greenpeace boat could count on being refueled there.

Despite these shortcomings, we were delighted that the DMAWC had chartered another vessel. The new Cannikin test date was November 4th. The *Greenpeace Too* had ample time to make it to Amchitka; the *Greenpeace* could not. On the other hand, there was also a sense of disappointment. Given the announced 8-day lead time, we could easily have reached Amchitka from Sand Point had we still been anchored there. From where we were, in the Georgia Strait, it would take the *Greenpeace* at least 12 days to reach Amchitka. As far as we knew, the AEC had not considered that we might have a second strike capability. At 18 miles per hour cruising speed, the *Greenpeace Too* could make it to Amchitka, from Vancouver, in a little over five days.

It was with mixed emotions that we docked alongside the *Greenpeace Too* at the wharf in Union Bay, B.C. After some hours of visiting the crew and Captain Johansen, I took down the Greenpeace flag from the *Greenpeace* and with due ceremony and some tears, handed it over to Johansen. The two of us hoisted the flag to the masthead of the *Edgewater Fortune*.

Once Terry Simmons, Bob Cummings, Rod Marining, and Dave Birmingham transferred to the *Greenpeace Too*, the sleek craft backed up a few hundred yards, and then, with a great revving of its powerful engines, stirred up a huge wake as it headed up the Georgia Strait for the northern end of Vancouver Island. There it cleared Cape Scott and headed out across the North Pacific on a great circle course for Amchitka. For those of us who stayed aboard the *Greenpeace,* the direct action campaign was over. We headed for home.

CHAPTER 3

GREENPEACE IS BEAUTIFUL

The meeting of the *Greenpeace* and the *Greenpeace Too* at the Union Bay wharf made for a rather unanticipated coincidence for me: Denman Island, the site of our new home was only one mile across Baynes Sound from the wharf.

In 1971, my father had died leaving my mother to run the family farm. I knew it was a matter of time before mother would sell. The family had always had a farm, and not having a land base made me feel at a lost. Just before my father's death, in 1970, Marie and I had vacationed, by automobile, across the Canadian heartland all the way east to Prince Edward Island. We had been on the lookout for farmland, but had found nothing that met both our needs and our pocketbooks. Then, in early 1971, we found a parcel of farmland on Denman Island, located off the east coast of Vancouver Island: 40 acres, in second and third growth forest, and another 20 acres that had been cleared and cultivated for hay—no buildings. The final purchase had been negotiated just days before I had left on the *Greenpeace* for Amchitka.

On October 30th, 1971, at 7:30a.m., the *Greenpeace* docked at the same False Creek pier from where we had set out, six weeks and four days before. As soon as the boat was secured, we abandoned ship. We wanted only to be reunited with our loved ones. I found Marie in the crowd that had gathered to greet us. We embraced, joined arms, and with not so much as a glance back, walked away from the pier, to the parked car, and home.

The next Monday morning, November 1st, I returned to work at the UBC Forest Products Laboratory. I walked in the front door, checked in with the receptionist, and walked down the glassed-in connecting corridor towards my office. On the way I met one of my colleagues. He was all smiles, congratulating me on the success of the voyage, and ended with, "Well Jim, what are you going to do next." Suddenly overcome with a great weariness, I replied, "Bob, what are *you* going to do next?"

Those few words summed up the essence of the campaign. Our job had been to make the people of North America aware of the real, and potential, danger of testing nuclear weapons. We imagined massive public opinion raging against the Cannikin underground blast and bringing about, once and for all, an end to the mad escalation of nuclear weapons. The *Greenpeace* and its crew had done its job.

Interest and concern now turned to the voyage of the *Greenpeace Too*, to Captain Johansen, and his crew. Although there was plenty of time to get to Amchitka to witness the test blast, circumstances arose that raised some doubt as to whether the *Greenpeace Too* would get there at all.

Soon after heading out into the North Pacific the reality of the *Edgewater Fortune's* basic instability was experienced. Many of the crew became violently ill. Then trouble occurred with one of the engines. So serious were the problems, that the boat had to go back to Prince Rupert for repairs and refueling. As well, crewmen, for whom seasickness was the most severe, left the ship, trip over. By the time engine repairs were made, the November 4th deadline was close at hand.

Leaving Prince Rupert for a direct run across the North Pacific, the *Greenpeace Too* ran into brutal weather. The engines were revved up, but the fierce storm drove them backwards. The Captain had no choice but to take the Inside Passage route.

After stopping at Juneau, the boat re-fueled for the long dash to Amchitka *via* the Gulf of Alaska. At the hour the bomb was to be exploded, the *Greenpeace Too* was still 1400 miles away. But the weather was clear, the ocean smooth, and the vaunted speed of the converted minesweeper was about to be tested. The formal appeal of the environmental and peace groups was partially successful: the test date was further postponed by two days. *Greenpeace Too* revved up its powerful engines to drive the boat at 22 knots. Still, at that pace, it was almost certain they would not reach Amchitka in time; at best they would arrive on November 7th, one day after the blast.

On November 6th, the U.S. Supreme Court defeated the appeal; AEC exploded the bomb. Cannikin went off with a power equivalent to 5 million tons of dynamite—the largest underground explosion conducted to date. The AEC was so convinced that the explosion was safe, that its Chairman James Schlesinger and his children had been flown to Amchitka for a picnic on the day of the test. Schlesinger neglected to mention that he and his family would be behind a mountain inside a massive concrete bunker mounted on heavy duty steel springs to absorb the shock.

The press onboard were greatly disappointed; the *Greenpeace Too* had not reached its objective in time. It, too, returned to Vancouver, crew despondent. But like the *Greenpeace* before it, the public education value of the campaign was enormous.

Headlines in the mainstream press trumpeted the success of the test: no tidal waves, no escape of radiation, no earthquakes. Their exuberance felt premature and short-sighted, and, was not supported by the long term reality of the blast. As well, it had been touch and go for the engineers and scientists at Amchitka. They had doubted whether or not they could successfully explode the bomb; the test hole had been filling with water at a rate faster than they could pump it dry. This had been caused by the rain that fell with increasing intensity as autumn progressed. This unforeseen circumstance destabilized the testing process, making the whole site a poor choice. By forcing the issue through the courts, so many delays had been imposed on the AEC, nature herself, nearly caused Cannikin to be canceled. There was also some evidence that the bomb's power had been reduced from 5 megatons, to 3.5 megatons. This was noted by University of Victoria seismologists when they measured the blast with their sensitive instruments.

I think that the AEC, and other Government agencies in the U.S., in seeing the powerful lobby developing against nuclear testing, opted for a blast of lesser force rather than face the consequences of something going wrong with the more powerful bomb that had been announced. I also think that the Greenpeace campaign had greatly influenced the outcome: four months after Cannikin, the AEC announced that it was abandoning its Amchitka Island nuclear test facility "for political and other reasons."

The crater from the Cannikin blast is one and one-half miles wide and 60 feet deep. Despite an AEC cover-up, researchers from the University of Alaska, at Fairbanks found that more than 1000 sea otters perished in the explosion. The numbers of other sea creatures such as seal, seabird, and fish, lost as a result of the explosion, are not known. According to Dan O'Neill of the University of Alaska,

> The bomb blast lifted the earth with such force that shorebirds
> standing on the beach above the explosion had their legs driven up
> into their bodies. The eyeballs of otters and seals burst through
> their skulls from the over-pressure caused in the ocean.

Samples of surface waters flowing from a creek that leads into the Bering Sea, just downstream from the test site, were gathered by Greenpeace scientists in 1996. The specimens indicated the presence of Americium-241, a radioactive product emanating from decaying plutonium. A speck of plutonium, if inhaled, can cause lung cancer. Amchitka remains, forever, a leaking legacy of decaying, poisonous, radioactive particles, posing a health hazard to whatever makes the North Pacific their home.

In 1973, the oil crisis dominated the political scene. The Organization of Petroleum Exporting Countries (OPEC) formed a cartel that created an artificial shortage of oil. Many nations of the world were net importers of oil; OPEC had the industrial world by the throat. Oil shortages illustrated how dependent we were on imported oil. In California, automobiles and trucks were lined up for hours at gas stations to fill their tanks and whatever other containers people could stuff into their vehicles. Facing such demand, many stations ran out of fuel while lines of vehicles kept on coming. Heated arguments developed, shootings were reported. The inability to satisfy energy needs is the Achilles heel of an industrial society.

The establishment, taken by surprise by OPEC, woke up to the fact that energy supply was the most critical element of our society. R. King Hubbard from the U.S. Geological Survey, had for many years predicted almost to the exact time, when energy consumption would exceed discoveries of new sources for oil. At that critical juncture, it would be a matter of a few decades before oil scarcity would be a real future instead of an artificial construct manufactured by the oil cartel.

In this state of affairs, it occurred to me that oil shortages just might be the wake up call we needed to become more energy self-reliant. To achieve this, we had to first become efficient in whatever energy source was employed currently. We then had to learn how to exploit renewable sources locally. Energy independence would be a binding force in shaping the new pioneering community I was beginning to envision.

Back to the Land: The Greenpeace Experimental Farm
It was becoming clear that soon I would have to make a fundamental lifestyle change. A once in a lifetime opportunity was presenting itself to create a living example of a successful ecologically and socially appropriate alternative, driven to popularity by the implications of an energy short world. As a research scientist I had gained experience in doing detailed background work concerning whatever it was that I

intended to investigate. Fortunately for me, my direct supervisor at the Forest Products Laboratory was sympathetic. This progressive attitude made it possible for me to search bodies of literature that dealt with energy. And oddly, in a rather synergistic manner, energy related subjects became interwoven with my formal research activities.

For instance, the Buckminster Fuller geodesic dome structures were inherently energy efficient, for their spherical shape enclosed the most volume per unit of surface area. A sphere can be heated with much less energy than can a cube of equal volume, all else in the structure being equal. I had worked with Fuller during the mid-1950s on the Distant Early Warning (DEW) system's microwave antenna housings: domes, 50 feet in diameter, constructed of fiberglass reinforced plastic. They were both weather proof and transparent to microwave communication signals. Twenty years later, in 1973, the Forest Products Laboratory was asked by the Capital Regional District to investigate the failure, under a two-inch snow load, of an owner built geodesic house structure on Salt Spring Island, situated off the east coast of Vancouver Island, near Victoria.

I was assigned to look into the problem and to suggest a construction method that would assure structural integrity. But you didn't need to be a rocket scientist to figure out what went wrong. Low on funds, not being able to afford the necessary bolts and steel required to ensure even minimal structural strength, the people who built the dome had fastened the structural elements together with flattened tin cans nailed onto wood 2x4s at the intersection where the webs of the geodesic dome are formed into its spherical shape. It was a wonder that the dome stood up during construction.

Based on the experience of the Salt Spring Island dome, the Regional District building inspector had wanted to write off domes, making them illegal to build within the Capital Regional District. However, this was the year of the global energy crisis (1973), and the development of geodesic dome homes could save energy. Energy conservation was also a part of the Canadian National Energy Plan, an official Federal Government policy. I was an employee of the Federal Government, and the laboratory where I worked was a Federal facility; it made great sense that I be given the assignment of designing and developing wood-framed geodesic dome components that were structurally sound, and, affordable.

At about the same time, a report had been issued by the Canadian Forest Service stating that the availability of Douglas-fir, the most popular species of construction lumber, would, by 1990, be in short supply. This was astonishing and frightening news. The forests of Canada, and especially those of British Columbia, were thought to be infinite and inexhaustible. The industry went into a state of denial, attempting to discredit the substance of the report. As the advance projects researcher in our laboratory, I brought this information to the attention of the laboratory director. Another project was added to my list: find a wood-based substitute for structural Douglas-fir. I investigated and came up with a possible design solution: laminated-veneer lumber.

The Forest Products Laboratory was located on the campus of the University of British Columbia. I had been introduced to the dean of the School of Architecture, and in the course of becoming familiar with my work on geodesic domes and engineered lumber, he expressed interest in doing some kind of cooperative research project involving the students, while at the same time, adding to the science of wood engineering.

Several students elected to take on the fabrication of a geodesic dome made from laminated-veneer structural components. My laboratory agreed to build the required molds and presses and to make available whatever laboratory facilities might be required. The effort resulted in a 32 foot diameter geodesic spherical space framework mounted on a 'tee' which made it resemble a gigantic golf ball. The unique structure was used by commercial airline pilots as a visual confirmation on their descent into Vancouver Airport. We didn't know of this until some years later when the structure was removed and the airport flight control people voiced their disappointment.

Meanwhile, I designed a low cost structurally reliable connector for geodesic dome-home builders that suited the technicians at the Capital Regional District. To further prove the design, Russ Chernoff, of the architecture school built a 16-foot diameter dome using my design. I fabricated the components for one of these domes in my Vancouver home workshop. Bill Darnell, the person who gave Greenpeace its name, his wife Elaine, Marie and I, trucked the geodesic dome components to our Denman Island property where we erected it in three days in May, 1972. That summer, Marie and I shingled the dome, installed windows and a door, and moved in. We lived in that cabin for a good portion of the three years it took us to build our permanent home on the Denman Farm.

The work with geodesic domes and engineered lumber was to be my final contribution to the research output of the Forest Products Laboratory. In 1974, I resigned, sold our home in Vancouver, and headed to Denman Island, there to establish our ecologically sustainable community.

The research work that I had done on low energy-use lifestyles led me to write a text entitled, *The New Pioneer's Handbook: Getting Back to the Land in an Energy-Scarce World*. The object of the book was to explain, in lay terms, the relation between energy use and ecological sustainability. At the same time this book was being written, there appeared in the literature a study which illustrated how to convert every manmade object into energy equivalents. This was accomplished by evaluating each object in terms of the energy used to extract the materials from the Earth, transporting them to the factory and converting them to the finished product, and estimating the amount of energy required to operate the object from its first to its last use.

To establish some relevance to this concept of energy accounting, I thought it would be useful, and interesting, to find what amount of energy could be employed forever in ways which preserves the integrity of the Earth's ecosystems. Several researchers have, over the past quarter century, addressed this task and they all conclude that about one billion people can be supported 'forever' at the current energy-use of the average North American. By 2050, the Earth's population is expected to be eight billion. At current energy-use rates, we would need to find eight more Earth-like planets to fulfill the need. A catastrophic prognosis.

I drew up what I called the 'world-around equitable energy resource use budget.' It was derived entirely from renewable sources of energy and from materials that were either renewable or, like sand from which to make glass, was in unlimited supply. It evaluated the various components of the 'good life' (as we North Americans have achieved), and it offered ecologically appropriate equivalents at vastly reduced energy use. It was my hope that the book would serve as a guide to help illustrate how a good life for eight billion people could be achieved within, what we call today, the carrying capacity of the Earth.

The New Pioneer's Handbook was published by Schocken Books of New York City, in the spring of 1975. The critics praised it widely; sales exceeded expectations. Schocken Books was the same book company that published all of Helen and Scott Nearing's extremely popular books, especially their best seller *Living the Good Life*. I was honored by the Nearings when, some years later, they named my book as one of the top ten of literally hundreds of books written about the 'back to the land movement' of the mid-60s and 70s.

In those early days financial resources were nonexistent. In order to generate some revenue, Marie and I had bought a run-down 'handyman's special' house in Courtenay, B.C.—a ferry ride and a few miles north of Denman Island. Our intention was to go full speed ahead on our Denman home, and at the same time do the work on the Courtenay house, so that when we moved to Denman, we could rent it. We moved into the Courtenay house in April of 1974, and stayed there until September 1977.

Early in 1974, while still at the Forest Products Laboratory, I had received a visit from a graduate biology student, Tom Lang. Tom had been a pre-med student at the University of Michigan. He was in his early twenties, and because he had dropped out of pre-med, he was eligible for the United States draft. The Vietnam War was still going on, and Tom, not wanting to serve, had emigrated to Canada in 1972. We discussed our project on Denman Island, his interest in organic agriculture, and his attraction to our plan of establishing an ecologically appropriate alternative lifestyle.

Tom made the move to Denman Island in late summer of 1974. With no capital to spare, and only a small income, Tom needed a roof over his head, and quickly. He had almost no experience as a house builder, so we had to come up with a design that was affordable, and simple to construct. This challenge led to my designing the Eco-Cabin, which was essentially a first order manifestation of a true geodesic dome. This cabin was built at a material cost of $200.

At around the same time, my son Lance, who had recently graduated from high school in Philadelphia where he lived with his mother, decided he wanted to live on the Denman farm, as well. Lance arrived just after Tom began construction. Lance had considerable house remodeling experience, and he knew his way around woodworking hand tools. Together, Lance and Tom built an Eco-Cabin for each of them. They were under roof just in time to face the first winter on the farm, ensconced in primitive but comfortable quarters. During the winter of 1974-75, we worked on the structural details of what was to be named the Greenpeace Experimental Farm. That year I spent designing our Denman Island house, remodeling the Courtenay house, and spending as much time as possible at the Greenpeace Farm.

Marie and I paid Tom and Lance $100 each a month. They, in turn, supplemented that income by picking oysters (Denman Island is known as the 'oyster capital of the world'), and by delivering the mail, in rural areas, for Canada Post.

As Tom and Lance were busy with completing their homes, Lance agreed to keep a daily record of their building as it progressed. We thought other people might be interested in this kind of structure and have need of a step-by-step instruction manual on how to build their own Eco-Cabin.

We produced the manual and had several hundred copies printed as a first run production. I sent complimentary copies of *The Eco-Cabin* to almost every 'do-it yourself' and 'back to the land' magazine I could find. Two reviewed the manual.

The *Harrowsmith Reader Source Book* printed a photo of the cover and gave a short summary of the contents. As well, the *Popular Science* magazine mentioned it in a very small article of about three column inches. That one mention generated a few thousand mail orders for the manual. Our self-publishing venture earned us enough money to buy two old Ford tractors, materials to build a good sized barn/workshop, and an assortment of badly needed garden tools.

To this day, more than twenty years since the publication of *The Eco-Cabin,* I still get enquiries concerning the availability of this construction manual. Several hundred copies of *The Eco-Cabin* were sold from the Greenpeace office in Vancouver—proceeds donated to Greenpeace.

With the publicity generated by the publication of *The New Pioneer's Handbook* and *The Eco-Cabin,* public interest in the Greenpeace Experimental Farm grew. More and more people were interested in the energy related development of rurally based ecologically appropriate lifestyles. Letters requesting information arrived daily.

In the spring of 1975, we prepared the groundwork for the foundation of our house. It was to be 600 square feet made up of two linked 20-foot diameter geodesic domes. One dome was for cooking and eating, and the other for relaxing and sleeping. By September, we had the basic shell of the structure under roof. During construction we lived half time in the small geodesic dome cabin that we assembled in 1972. I commuted to the house site on Denman each day, picking up and transporting a load of building materials in our Datsun truck. Tom and

Lance helped with assembling the dome components which I had pre-fabricated in the basement of the Courtenay house.

Green Movement Roots

It was proving difficult to dedicate full time to building our house on Denman; there always seemed to be some important issue that required my participation. One of these issues got me involved in local politics.

Marie and I had joined a local environmental group: Citizen's Planning Action Committee (CPAC). It was headed by Fran Johnson, the Courtenay Library chief librarian. She was committed to bringing a halt to the rampant growth that was plunging Courtenay and the surrounding farmland into strip malls. One of the most vocal promoters of expansion for the sake of expansion was the mayor, Bill Moore. Moore's father was the first New Democratic Party member elected to Parliament in Ottawa. His democratic-socialist leanings generated working class support for him and his son Bill. Bill Moore was returned unopposed for five consecutive two-year terms as mayor of Courtenay.

In 1974, the City had been approached by two different developers of shopping malls. Each mall was to be located just outside the city boundaries, but they needed to hook into the city sewage treatment system, and to accomplish this their land had to be incorporated *within* city boundaries. To justify this capital expense there had to be some 'reason' given to the city councilors. CPAC learned that Mayor Moore had been flown to Edmonton, Alberta, by one of the developers to examine a similar mall project which featured a Zeller's Department Store. At the other end of town the Dominion Bridge company had approached the City with plans to develop another mall. Its construction, if allowed, would mean the paving over of acres and acres of Class-1 farmland.

CPAC undertook this issue with a campaign against both malls. They claimed, that if built, the city core, which afforded people easy walking access to most stores and services, would soon disappear, increasing dependency on the automobile. It was decided that we would oppose the Mayor's bid for re-election with a CPAC endorsed candidate; that candidate was me.

I ran on a controlled population growth platform. If elected I would not permit any extension of the city boundaries until the existing building lots were developed. This plan would enable the City to gradually extend the sewer, water, schools, and municipal functions: to expand at a more organic rate of growth. I opposed both malls on grounds that they were each more than a mile from the business core, and would have cost the City huge outlays of tax money to provide the services infrastructure.

The Mayor countered with the standard argument that growth is good, and that if you opposed growth you were un-Canadian, and probably a Communist. I had the support of CPAC, of course, and I gained editorial support from one of the local newspapers, *The Island Star*. Phil Frost, the editor, and Murray Davidson, the paper's staff photographer, went all out with a series of feature articles in the *Star* aimed at building a voter base for my campaign.

On election day, four weeks after the campaign began, my supporters were confident, optimistic, and enthusiastic, but I didn't share their enthusiasm. I was worried that perhaps I would win. Then what. All I had wanted was to move to Denman Island, and, as soon as possible.

As it turned out, the Mayor incumbent was re-elected; I received 17 percent of the vote. But it occurred to me that if I, running as an independent, offering an alternative to the hallowed growth syndrome, could get as much electoral support as I did, what kind of support could be generated with an organized formal political party. The seed for green politics was planted.

It was too bad for Courtenay that the city councilors did not follow the lead of the Citizens Planning Action Committee. Today, some twenty years later, the City has both malls, a declining city core, an enormous traffic build-up, a big-city crime problem, and a rapidly increasing tax burden. Visually, Courtenay is a victim of the strip development that plagues most mid-sized cities across North America: just plain ugly.

The election campaign over, I was looking forward to completing the Denman house and moving there within the next few months. That was not to be. In February of 1976, I answered a knock on the door of our Courtenay home. Opening it, I found two tall, husky, bearded men. I thought they were either robbers, hippies, or RCMP in disguise, about to persecute us for harboring draft-dodgers. It turned out they worked for the Liberal Party, and were on a Government preparatory committee for the United Nations' sponsored Habitat Conference on Human Settlements slated to be held in Vancouver during June of 1976. They had heard of my work with alternative housing, and had come to ask if I would take on the job of managing the UN conference site which would display working examples of alternative buildings. The exhibit would be in Jericho Park, on the ocean at English Bay, in the heart of Vancouver. My old acquaintance Bucky Fuller would be there, as well as Margaret Mead, and Paulo Soleri—a host of luminaries with hands-on experience in building alternative housing.

On the one hand, answering this call would provide us with the finances needed to complete the Denman house, but on the other hand, I could kiss May and June good-bye. Our move to Denman was once more delayed.

I had a wonderful time. The official conference, held in a dreary downtown Vancouver skyscraper, accomplished little. Most of the delegates, who were from nations around the world, spent their time at the Habitat Forum by the sea. Architects and engineers worked to make certain their building projects were on time for the opening. In less than a month, a village of alternative housing, of special interest to delegates from third-world nations, was built. The housing exhibits ran the full gamut: from the latest state-of-the-art energy efficient construction, to a building made entirely from the remains of a theoretical post-nuclear war site. Architecture students from the University of British Columbia prefabricated an entire house made from sandwiches of plywood and styrofoam, cleverly designed so that it could be assembled without written instruction or need of previous building experience.

Another landmark project was a family sized cabin made entirely from firewood length wood logs cemented together with sawdust-reinforced concrete mortar. This structure was expressly designed for the extreme cold of the Canadian North. Cree Indians, sponsored by the University of Manitoba in Winnipeg, traveled from Manitoba to Vancouver as volunteer construction workers. About thirty buildings constituted the Habitat Forum instant town. I had the privilege of escorting Pierre Trudeau, the, then, Prime Minister of Canada, through the site. (It had pleased me that Prime Minister Trudeau, at the time of the Greenpeace initiative against the Amchitka nuclear testing, had sent a telegram in support.)

From my viewpoint the most interesting aspect of the Habitat Forum exhibits were the alternate energy equipment: particularly, the electricity producing windmills. There were five different styles. One was from the National Research Council of Canada. They had developed a wind turbine that stood upright; it looked like a giant eggbeater, mounted vertically, and attached to a platform on the ground. Another was a Quirk's propeller windmill from Australia, and yet another, a homemade propeller type from a commune in the United States.

Common to them all, sadly, was the fact that not one produced even a kilowatt of electricity. For the whole month that the exhibits stood in Jericho Park, there simply was no wind of sufficient force to produce enough power to spin the generators. To a technophile, and as one intent on creating an infrastructure of self-reliance, the non-performance of these sophisticated wind machines was quite a blow. I had had visions of clean, cheap, power from wind, producing at least some of the Farm's energy requirements. Now, it seemed, if the wind didn't blow, I would have to depend on fossil-fuel generation of electric power as a backup. I was aware that steady wind availability would go a long way towards making the wind generated electric power production practical. I had learned this while researching and writing *The New Pioneer's Handbook*. Most of my source material had been from the early 1930s; I had thought by now, in the 1970s, the machines being exhibited at the Habitat Forum would have solved the technological problems incurred by low wind speed wind/electric power production. Obviously, it had not.

I made many acquaintances at the United Nations conference. David Satterthwait, the director of Habitat Forum was both a joy to work with and to share ideas with. Leslie Adams, of Canada World Youth, served as a volunteer and led scores of groups of young people through the Forum exhibits. I was impressed by this young woman's enthusiasm, energy and knowledge of third-world problems and their need for assistance from the wealthier nations. The Habitat Forum was also the venue for the launch of the latest voyage to save the whales. It was the *James Bay* renamed the *Greenpeace VII*, with thirty crew-members dedicated to placing themselves between the Soviet whaling fleet's harpoons and their quarry, the scarce great whales that roamed the Pacific Ocean.

Again, a convergence brought about by the launch of a Greenpeace campaign and the beginnings of a global movement addressing ecological concerns that affect a rapidly growing human population. And, these concerns were being addressed in Vancouver where Greenpeace had been born.

Survival on the Farm

After the experiences at Habitat Forum I was more determined than ever to complete the Denman house and move to the Farm. Once more, fate intervened. As the Denman home neared completion, Marie and I began a search for a decent stove. We had plenty of windfall trees on our property that would provide for our fuel needs. We contacted everybody that offered woodstoves for sale, but most stoves proved ugly or inefficient. We wanted both beauty and efficiency. Finally, after much research, we located a stove called Jotul, made in Norway, available from a heating contractor in New Westminster, a suburb of Vancouver. It was love at first sight. The Jotul stove was cast iron, clean in design, and fuel efficient. We bought three: one for Marie and I, one for Tom and one for Lance.

We put them under the canopy of our Datsun pickup for the long trip back to Denman Island. While waiting in the ferry line-up at the Denman Island commuter ferry terminal, an acquaintance who was also waiting for the ferry, peeked into the Datsun and saw the stoves. He asked if he could take a closer look. I opened the canopy, let down the tailgate, and slid one forward. Suddenly, the truck was surrounded by people, fellow Denman Islanders, asking about cost and availability.

The owner of the New Westminster store had told me he wasn't interested in selling the stoves any longer, but encouraged by the interest of the onlookers at the ferry terminal, I took the plunge, and told them I would try to find a place where the Jotul could be bought.

My search led to a Montreal importer, Deluxe Equipment. In telephone conversation with the sales manager, Mederil Tremblay, I was told I could become a dealer by placing an order for five stoves. I gave him the order. Three weeks later, when I picked them up at the freight depot, three of the five stoves had already been sold. When I delivered them to Denman Island, the same ferry line-up phenomenon occurred. The two remaining stoves also sold. That night over supper, I said to Marie, "Looks like we're in the woodstove business."

Over the next three years we did an incredible amount of business selling and installing wood heating equipment. First under the name of Woodstoves Unlimited, and then a distribution division with participating partners in a corporate entity known as Pacific Conserver Products. We sold thousands of stoves, and opened up retail stores in Courtenay, in Vancouver, and in Duncan, on Vancouver Island. Tom moved to Vancouver to manage the store there; Lance became chief installer, and, reluctant salesperson, at the Courtenay store. One of our partners managed the Duncan store. I handled the group purchasing and did the basic importing and selling to the ten distributors we had established in British Columbia and Alberta. But none of us had been prepared for the time and commitment that the woodstove business required, and in 1981 we decided to close down.

Despite the distraction of running the woodstove business, the Greenpeace Farm was taking shape. In September of 1977, Marie and I had moved to Denman to live full time. We established a large organic garden, fenced to eight feet in height to keep the deer out. Tom, Lance, and a number of volunteers built a traditional west coast barn which we used as a machine shop and activity center for the folks that visited and worked on the Farm. So many people were interested in what we were doing, we decided to take on volunteer workers for short term internships.

From the beginning, we had nothing but problems. We were obliged to set up rules, but this did not work very well, and we came to realize that we were doomed to fail. We soon gave up on the idea; instead, we would enhance what we were already doing on the Greenpeace Experimental Farm. We decided to specialize in the development of the technical infrastructure for achieving ecologically sustainable lifestyles, document them, and make them available to whomever was interested. We had already developed energy-efficient housing, created biological waste disposal systems, and designed and built a highly productive organic garden, greenhouses, and solar heated shower system.

Woodgas

The next energy-related task confronting us was to come up with a viable renewable resource alternative to the use of fossil fuels to power the internal combustion engine. Specifically, the design, construction, and evaluation of a tractor to do farm work and a road vehicle to operate on public roads in performance of essential services. While working at the Forest Products Laboratory, in Vancouver, I had met Dr. Clive Dayson, head of the National Research Council Mechanical Engineering Laboratory. He was involved with George McRobie who ran the Appropriate Technology Foundation after Fritz Schumacher died. Shumacher was the author of the bestseller *Small is Beautiful*. I first met McRobie at the Habitat Forum, where we discussed various scenarios concerning what projects would be most apt to advance the art of a new engineering principle called Appropriate Technology (AT).

The practitioners of appropriate technology, or AT as it is also known, were interested in finding ways that would enable people in underdeveloped nations to build devices and implements that could be made from local materials, were energy efficient, economical, and easy to use and repair.

One example of AT was an energy-efficient cookstove made of clay and sundried bricks that used less than half the amount of wood fuel consumed by traditional cooking stoves. Another was a hand-operated deep well pump made from ordinary water pipe and locally available materials for the plunger and packing. The stove and pump were widely used throughout rural Africa, making life more pleasant, and healthier, for thousands of residents.

Dayson believed that industrialized countries also needed to use the design approach of AT, even though a more complex level of technology was available, and was inexpensive. Always mindful that farmer's out of pocket costs were rising, due to rapidly increasing oil prices, I knew they would be interested in less expensive alternative fuels.

In *The New Pioneers Handbook,* there was a section on woodgas powered vehicles. There, I suggested that an ecologically appropriate way to fuel tractors and automobiles would be to use waste wood and/or surplus crop residues, such as corn cobs. By utilizing the gasifier technology employed extensively in Europe during World War II, and incorporating an AT approach to the design, a meaningful contribution to the nation's economy might be realized, as the energy cost savings would filter down from the farmer to the citizenry in the form of lower food prices.

The development of this technology would require considerable bench testing of the components. A full scale demonstration prototype would have to be built for field trials. We submitted an application for funding to the National Research Council in the amount of $10,000. Dr. Dayson indicated his willingness to oversee the woodgas project. The grant was approved.

At the Habitat Forum, I had also met Rob Longley, a young engineering technician from England. He was intending to build a woodgas generator to power his automobile as a student project. I invited him to join us on the Greenpeace Farm where he could live and do some work on our woodgas tractor project. He agreed.

Since wood waste is by far the most available fuel on Denman Island, we targeted our designs towards the conversion of wood to woodgas. The chemistry of converting wood to woodgas is straightforward. The wood is first burned in a controlled oxygen environment to become charcoal. The charcoal is further heated. The products of combustion are carbon dioxide and water. These combustion products are drawn through the bed of hot charcoal which is essentially pure carbon. The carbon dioxide is transformed to carbon monoxide and hydrogen. In turn, some of the hydrogen is converted to methane. The gasses, carbon monoxide, hydrogen, and methane are flammable and when mixed with about an equal volume of air, produces a combustible mixture. It is this gas mixture that is fed to the engine's intake manifold, then to the sparkplugs which ignite the gas, exploding to drive the pistons.

It is not widely known that carbon monoxide is a combustible fuel. Most know it as an odorless highly toxic gas. The woodgas mixture runs a standard internal combustion engine at about 70 percent of the power that it generates from gasoline fuel. The technical problem that confronts the designer of portable woodgas production centers is the need for converting wood to woodgas continuously, and in delivering it on demand to an internal combustion engine. Another problem is cleaning the gas of particulate matter before it enters the engine.

We designed the generator apparatus using readily available recycled components. It was constructed from a used 45-gallon can, assorted plumbing fittings, a war surplus fan, paint cans, and fiberglass insulation for the filter material. These components were fitted together and mounted on a Ford model 9N tractor. The first work done by Woodgas I, was relatively light. We used it to mow hay, and in a stationary mode, to pump water for irrigating the garden, and to charge a bank of batteries to power our electrical needs. Everything worked so well that our enthusiasm extended to another project. We fabricated a woodgas generator to fuel the engine of the Datsun pickup truck that we used to service the mail delivery route. Should this experiment be successful, we would be truly energy self-sufficient.

We thought a trip south to Arizona, where mountains, desert, snow, and heavy rains would all be encountered, would be a good test of the Datsun woodgas-equipped vehicle. Beforehand, several problems had to be resolved. The first had to do with obtaining an adequate supply of wood fuel. The engine consumed about one gallon of gasoline per hour; the energy equivalent of one gallon of gasoline is about 20 pounds of air dried wood. At an average speed of 50 mph, over a planned trip of 3,000 miles, about 60 hours worth of fuel would need to be packed onboard. The truck would have to carry 1,200 pounds of wood to accomplish the round trip without having to refuel. It could carry about 200 pounds, or 10 gallons, gasoline equivalent. But we did not anticipate much of a refueling problem. It was likely that scrap wood could be had from building supply houses encountered *en route*. Nevertheless, we assumed the worst condition of not being able to obtain a sure supply of wood, and rigged the engine to operate on gasoline as well. Where wood was not available, we could switch to gasoline fuel.

As previously described, the combustible wood fuel gas air mixture is introduced through the intake manifold, ignited by the spark plug, which produces the controlled explosion that in turn drives the engine's cylinders. The conventional gasoline/air mixture path is introduced to the engine in exactly the same way. With minor modifications to the carburetor the woodgas/air mixture and the gasoline/air mixture can function integrally. This means that either fuel mixture can be employed at the discretion of the operator. Two separate accelerator pedals were installed side by side on the floor of the Datsun truck.

During the trip to Arizona, the gasoline fuel mixture was used only when wood was not available, or when mountain roads required a power boost. For the 3,000 mile round trip, only 20 gallons of gasoline were used. Though few problems were encountered in the operation of the woodgas generator, we realized more work was required to find a better method for cleaning the woodgas: on the Arizona trip the filter had to be cleaned every fifty miles or so.

The details of construction for the woodgas system were recorded and a 'how-to' book complete with a set of plans entitled "Woodgas Plans" was produced. We distributed them by mail order in North America; hundreds were sold. Most of the plan purchasers were from the U.S., and most were interested in using crop wastes, such as straw, instead of wood, so we designed a handling system to accommodate their needs.

It occurred to me, much later, to ask myself how much wood it would take to fuel the planet's automobile and truck fleet. In ten years there would not be one tree left on the planet. This revelation shocked me.

CHAPTER 4

GREEN ACTION

For seven years, the Greenpeace Farm was not connected to the electric grid. Several 12-volt deep-cycle marine batteries, kept charged with a gasoline fueled portable 1,000 watt electrical generator, powered our home. We were able to meet all of our electricity requirements with 3 KWH generated per week. This compares with a utility-supplied residence which averages about 250 KWH per week. A small propane-powered refrigerator served our needs, and low wattage 12-volt bulbs provided the lighting. Wood-fired space heaters warmed the rooms. It occurred to us that our minimal use of fossil fuels to generate power for our needs was an exercise in futility and perhaps even counterproductive. Fossil fuels pollute.

To hook up to the electric grid would permit us to employ hydroelectric generated electricity from the vast river systems of British Columbia. Although we knew of the adverse ecological effects of large-scale hydro generation, we felt that on balance, it would be more ecologically appropriate. We hooked up to the grid, but with a continuing allegiance to conservation. Our electric bills were larger than anticipated: the less electricity used, the higher the rate charged. Clearly, the utilities were promoting greater use of energy, not conservation of it. The politics of energy generation and distribution were still in the domain of growth promoters.

For many years, I attended public meetings called by B.C. Hydro, the province's energy utility. These meetings were not gratuitous: the public demanded them. It was in the early 1970s; 'environmentalists' began to hold energy utilities accountable: first, for energy pricing, then, for energy conservation.

The mandate of the utilities was to sell as much electricity as possible. To do that, they gave the consumer incentive: the more energy used, the cheaper it would be. And, the utility people had no problem about supply: as demand grew, dam another river, or build a nuclear power plant or fossil fuel facility. There was very little appreciation of 'marginal cost pricing': costs required to provide new power, and/or to replace existing power plants. That would be charged to the consumer. It was only when marginal costs became exorbitant, that the utilities were interested in promoting energy conservation.

The nuclear option, analyzed from the perspective of safe disposal of high level wastes, introduced an uncertainty factor. The ensuing crisis of Three Mile Island and Chernobyl caused many utilities to simply give up their plans to build nuclear power facilities. The demise of a nuclear future was soon joined on another front. The enormous salmon fishing industry of the Pacific North West was endangered by a severe shortfall of Columbia River salmon, generally believed to have been caused in a failure of the system of fish ladders supposed to provide a migration route for adult salmon to reach their breeding places upstream of the river. As well, acid rain, primarily emanating from coal-fired electric generating stations, was killing fish in the lakes of the U.S., Canada, and Europe. Collectively, these occurrences placed growth constraints on the future of new electric generating facilities. The opportunities for expansion became limited, and it began to look as though conservation, rather than promotion, made better economic sense.

The Rocky Mountain Institute, under the direction of Amory Lovins, led the struggle to educate the utilities. The Institute maintained that at least 50 percent of generated electricity was wasted, and that energy consumption could be further reduced by energy-efficient design. In combination, it was claimed that 80 percent of generated electricity could be saved. This would release an enormous amount of present generating capability to serve the needs of home and industry at a much lower cost than if a growth oriented policy were to result in constantly having to build new generating facilities.

The move to energy efficiency, and energy conservation, would ease the pain of providing new generation facilities. However, with demands for energy by underdeveloped nations rapidly increasing, and further exacerbated by the unchecked growth of global populations, gains from conservation and design measures would, ultimately, result in a scarcity of energy supply. Recognizing this eventuality, it made sense to develop non-polluting new energy sources, now: when conventional sources were depleted, safe energy systems could be deployed.

It was at this point of transforming from a consumer to a conserver society, that I wondered what, if any, limits existed to the quantity of energy that could be derived from renewable ecologically-appropriate sources. I believed that there were limits, and that these limits were ever more rapidly being approached.

The Greens Organize

The notion of a 'green' politics took root in the environmental movement. The first organized political group was the Values Party of New Zealand, in 1972. At about the same time, in the United Kingdom, the Ecology Party was formed. By 1982, the German Green Party (Die Grunen), with 8 percent of the popular vote, had representation in Parliament. In 1980, having the goal of founding a Green Party of Canada, Mark Craft, from Alberta, and I, organized a meeting in Saskatoon, Saskatchewan, a province that had a history of embracing progressive political movements. At the time, the New Democratic Party was in power. Word had gotten out that we had intentions of forming a party of the environment; this was seen as an attempt to 'split the Left,' and a concerted effort was made to take over our meeting. They succeeded, preventing any serious move towards forming a new political party.

The first successful green political movement in North America, occurred in Vancouver, in the spring of 1983. Encouraged by the electoral success of the Die Grunen, a small group of Vancouverites, led by Adriane Carr, founded the Green Party of British Columbia. The Greens contested the upcoming election, and Carr received about 2 percent of the popular vote. This was encouraging: Carr had no previous experience, and the Green Party's platform suffered from a lack of specifics. The effort had, as well, given a political voice to concerns about the state of the British Columbia environment. The Greens had achieved a measure of respect from the electorate; in future, green values would have to be addressed by major political parties.

I joined the B.C. Greens in 1983. That same year, the, then, President of Greenpeace Canada and Canada's representative on the Greenpeace International Board of Directors, Dr. Patrick Moore, invited me to join the Greenpeace Canada Board of Directors.

Greenpeace Canada had been concentrating on animal rights and anti-pollution activities. Moore wanted me to set up an anti-nuclear campaign, and be its coordinator. I agreed to serve on the Board, but took a rain-check on actually working on campaigns. Then, in early 1984, I became a founding director of the Green Party of Canada and was involved with the upcoming Federal election. I helped to organize throughout Canada and agreed to stand for parliament in the Vancouver electoral district where I had previously lived: Vancouver-Point Grey. It was an upscale university liberal/conservative residential area; votes normally went to the Liberal Party. In the 1984 Federal election, the leader of the Liberals, John Turner, chose to run in the same district.

I, and my campaign coordinator, Seymour Trieger, agreed that it might be of some public interest if I campaigned house to house on my bicycle, which I was riding around Vancouver at that time. Point Grey residential areas are all laid out around the same land-use blueprint: lots are narrow and long, and houses close to the street, leaving space at the rear of the property for gardens and garages. These were accessed by lanes between properties that served as pickup points for garbage collectors, and, for the running of utility wires and other services. These back lanes were interesting: there, fruit trees overhung back fences, people strolled with dogs, men and women tended their gardens and chatted with their neighbors. I thought that knocking on the front door and attempting to put across the Green message, from that vantage point, would be difficult and awkward, but if I cruised the back lanes, then perhaps I stood a better chance of getting a green politics across.

The idea worked. The back fence conversations convinced many, but just as many candidly told me, although they supported my efforts, they were unable to vote for the Green Party. Their reasoning: They didn't want to waste their vote on a political party that had no chance of being elected. A classical Catch 22 situation: to influence the governance of Canada, the Greens would have to show support by the voters, but if the electorate wouldn't vote for the Green Party because they were not likely to gain a parliamentary presence, nobody would vote for a Green candidate. Clearly, a system of proportional representation would have to be in place, similar to the German electoral system, before the Green Party could expect the electorate to vote according to their conscience rather than strategically.

The prospects for such a system is dim, for a Catch 22 exists there also. In order to revise the electoral system, it has to become law. To become law, Parliament has to secure a majority vote. Since the majority of parliamentarians were elected by the existing system of 'first past the post,' they will not vote for a different system than the one which elected them. Recently, the UK introduced a new electoral system—a partial proportional representation system—that was used to elect the Mayor of London, and council. Canada, and the U.S., are among the few countries that remain electorally unchanged.

Greenpeace Calls

In 1982, the Canadian Government was asked by the United States Government for permission to flight test nuclear capable cruise missiles, that fly at treetop levels, over the boreal forest area of the Canadian north. In western Europe, hundreds of people were in the streets, and mounting security fences around cruise missile installations, in protest.

Greenpeace International was not particularly interested in campaigning actively against cruise missile testing. Technically, the cruise tests had nothing to do with the actual testing of a nuclear bomb, and, at that time, there was a, more or less, *defacto* ban on testing nuclear weapons. The Strategic Arms Limitation Treaty (SALT) negotiations were underway between the U.S. and the USSR, and any activity that tended to provoke was felt to be detrimental. But Canada's allowing the testing of nuclear weapons delivery systems at a time when a nuclear stand-down was being negotiated, could be seen to undermine the arms limitation negotiation process. The Greenpeace International Nuclear Campaign Coordinator, Gerd Liepold, agreed that Greenpeace Canada should make every effort to stop the cruise from being test flown.

There was, as well, considerable support among the Greenpeace Canada Board for additional Greenpeace action. They had already participated in the peace walks held in Vancouver, in Toronto, and in Victoria, where more than 100,000 people had walked in protest. Wanting to do more, the Board voted to help fund the Cold Lake Peace Camp; it was being set up, in protest, and, in solidarity with the United Kingdom's Women's Peace Camp at Greenham Common. I volunteered to act as liaison and went to Cold Lake to help organize, and to scout the best way to conduct a direct action against the cruise.

Flight testing consisted of an unarmed cruise missile released from a B-52 bomber high over the Beaufort Sea in the Canadian arctic. The cruise would fly south along the MacKenzie River, over the snow covered landscape, near the speed of sound, at an altitude of 300 feet. When reaching a point about 150 miles north of the city of Edmonton, the missile would turn east to land at the Primrose Lake Air Weapons Range, which straddled the Alberta/Saskatchewan border. All the tests were to be conducted during the months when snow covered the ground. The Cold Lake Peace Camp was to be our base of operation in the area.

During the winter of 1983, I flew to Calgary, where I met a Greenpeace member who volunteered to drive the 300 miles north to Cold Lake. It was the first time I had ever experienced the frigid north. The car was an ancient Austin sedan that could not deliver enough heat.

The tent peace camp, which had essentially disbanded at the first frost, was relocated for the winter in a rented house at the edge of town. During the day, the temperature outside rose to a high of -26F; at night, it sank to -48F. At this temperature, the only way to be sure your car would start in the morning, was to keep the engine running through the night.

We drove out to the road that was the only public entrance to the Primrose Lake Air Weapons Range. If we could block this road, the Canadian Forces personnel could not gain access to the range. If we could 'be there' at the time of the test, this might cause the test to be canceled. But blocking the road would not be the problem; the problem would be letting the world know what we were doing. Primrose Lake was far from Edmonton, the nearest media center.

What we knew was: the Canadian Government was going to sign a 5-year automatically renewable agreement with the United States giving permission to test unarmed cruise missiles; that the agreement was to be signed some time in mid-1983; and that the tests were to take place during the winter. We also knew, from the anti-war movement in Canada, that a mother's march from Edmonton to Cold Lake Peace Camp and then to Ottawa, was planned.

Then, we got the news that in the United Kingdom, the Greenham Commons Peace Camp had been invaded by the authorities: many people were arrested, several were hurt. Despite massive protests the cruise had been deployed in European NATO facilities. Pressure was building worldwide on the issue of cruise deployment. I had the job of doing an action against the cruise tests that would attract the media and further rouse the public to protest Canada's contribution to this missile system that would destabilize the arms limitation talks.

It had been twelve years since I had led a Greenpeace campaign. The Vancouver office was located in trendy Kitsilano, over a ground floor fitness studio. The small office staff consisted of four paid employees, plus several volunteers who worked as needed. Greenpeace Vancouver also supervised operations in Alberta, and it was from these Albertan Greenpeacers that I selected the action team that would block the only access road to the Canadian Forces Base at Primrose Lake. In view of the possibility that the media would not show up for a road blockade, Greenpeace Toronto organized a direct action at the Parliament buildings in Ottawa. The two actions were to be simultaneous.

On June 22nd, Greenpeacers from Toronto left for Ottawa, and the Greenpeace Alberta team met in Edmonton. We borrowed the Greenpeace van from Edmonton, and at 3:00a.m. headed northeast for Primrose Lake. We rendezvoused at the Cold Lake Peace Camp, then drove towards the Primrose Lake access road.

In Ottawa, at 9:00a.m., Dan McDermott and Karen Pierce chained themselves to the doors of Parliament. At exactly the same time, 7:00a.m. in Alberta, Kevin McKeown, Annette Ruitenbeek, David Dawes and myself, cuffed ourselves to a chain that stretched across the width of the road. Our objective: to block access to the day shift of personnel who worked at the test range.

In Ottawa, the media were handed a Greenpeace press release describing the dual actions. At Primrose Lake, twenty or so media vehicles pulled to the side of the road and set up cameras. RCMP arrived, and parked some distance away, making no attempt, at least for the moment, to remove us.

The Primrose Lake day shift never appeared. We had noticed helicopters flying over us, to and from the test facility. After a few hours of standing unchallenged on the road, we realized that the military had been flying the day shift in and airlifting the night shift out. Later in the day, we heard the sound of a heavy machine crashing through the woods not far from us; the military had bulldozed a bypass around the blockaded area. Their strategy, and that of the RCMP, was to not challenge the blockade, but to go over, or, around it.

As the day wore on, the June heat increased. The bugs began to bite; we, nevertheless, hung in, not quite sure what to do next. The media interviewed us, took pictures, and began to pack up their gear to go home. As afternoon turned into evening, and we were still chained across the road, George Callies, who had been steadfastly providing us with food, suggested that we remove our blockade. We had proved our point: the Ottawa chain-in had made the national news.

Despite widespread protests, and despite our twin actions, late in the afternoon of July 15th, 1983 (what was to be known as Black Friday), the Canadian Government signed the agreement with the U.S. Government to allow the testing of unarmed cruise missiles in Canadian air space, and the use of ground facilities at Primrose Lake.

The Cruise Catcher

In the closing weeks of 1984, the Greenpeace office received a brown envelope containing a detailed terrain map. It identified the course to be followed for each flight test—exactly the same course, each time. We reasoned that we might be able to locate a point along the flight path where the missile crossed accessible public land. Luanne Roth, the comptroller of Greenpeace Canada, suggested we erect a barrage balloon to float up in the air and actually intercept the missile, forcing it to take evasive measures. This unanticipated interference with the test process would undoubtedly confuse the cruise sufficiently to make the flight data useless to the military.

The Amchitka energy was once again unleashed. Undaunted by the immensity of the job—first locating, then forcing the missile off course—it wasn't long before we figured out just how we could do it.

Greenpeace had long been campaigning against drift-net fishing—a technique, developed with United Nations funding, intended to enable people of developing nations an affordable method for efficiently catching large numbers of fish. Fine, almost transparent filaments of a tough plastic were woven into huge, lightweight nets. Unfortunately, the worldwide commercial fishing fleet started using these enormous nets, often several miles long, and were fishing everything in sight.

We got hold of a piece of drift-net about 30 meters long, by 7 meters wide, and helium-filled meteorological balloons that we hoped would lift the net into the path of the cruise as it flew over Route 63, between Edmonton and Fort McMurray, near the town of Wandering River.

The netting weighed five pounds, including a sewn-on banner stretching the full width of the net: Stop Nuclear Testing Now. Six balloons, evenly spaced along its length should raise the netting to at least 300 feet. The contraption was constructed and flight-tested in a snow covered suburban Vancouver park, in early January 1985. A video of the net flight was made; it was also photo documented. The test was successful. The problem before us now, was how to locate precisely where the missile would cross Route 63.

Our budget could not support the acquisition of surveying equipment. I remembered that the pyramids of Egypt were constructed to an accuracy that at least equaled the precision of today's sophisticated measuring equipment. A trip to the library provided us with a detailed reproduction of the simple device used by Egyptian engineers in the days of the pharaohs.

A triangle can be constructed if one knows the length of one leg, and two of the angles adjacent to the one leg. The angle measurement is achieved using a fishing line sinker, a piece of string, and a triangular piece of thin plywood. The degrees of angular measurement is painted onto the surface of the plywood. The observer sights along the top of the plywood aiming at the missile flying as it crosses the highway. Then, holding the apparatus in place, allows the weighted string to seek its gravity induced vertical position. Where the string crosses the marked angular, indices are recorded. Another viewer, at the other end of the measured line, which is positioned exactly one mile down the road, would make a similar angular measurement. To locate where the cruise would cross the road was simple. Extend the two other sides of the triangle at the measured angles until they crossed. At the point of intersection, draw a line perpendicular to the base line, and where it intersects that line, represents the exact location of where the missile would cross the highway, and, at what altitude.

The military were intending to fly the test route with a B-52 bomber, tethering a cruise missile from its bomb bay, in a test of the cruises' inertial guidance system. Greenpeacers and representatives from other peace groups in northern Alberta were invited to witness the effort at pinpointing exactly where the cruise would cross Route 63. The net would also be deployed and test flown at that time.

Kevin McKeown headed up the Greenpeace team. They drove to the site in a van which left Vancouver loaded down with the net, balloons, bottles of helium, and the 'Cruise Finders' (as we named the triangulation devices).

The sun slowly crept over the horizon on this cold, clear, January day. The van took up its position along Route 63, and measured out one mile along the road. At each end of the ground line, Greenpeacers were poised to sight along their cruise finders. It was estimated that the B-52, with its cruise missile dangling underneath, would cross Route 63 about three hours from the beginning of its ranging south from its position over the Beaufort Sea.

As the team waited, they inflated the balloons, fastened them to the net, and lofted the net into the air. Nothing happened; the net would not rise. The very cold air had reduced the lifting capability. Larger, and perhaps more balloons, would be needed; the situation would be remedied by the time the free flight cruise tests were to begin.

The B-52 appeared on schedule, racing low over the horizon. It crossed a few feet from the center of the line that Greenpeace had laid out along the road. Information previously leaked to us about the flight path was accurate. We had accomplished what had been considered, by most, un-achievable: we located and mapped the exact flight path of the cruise missile.

Back in Vancouver, we got larger balloons and worked out a strategy for attracting a media presence along Route 63 at Wandering River. Up to now, we had not extended an invitation. We had not yet worked out exactly what we were going to do for the action against the upcoming test of the cruise—the free flight from the Beaufort Sea to a parachute-assisted soft landing at Primrose Lake Air Weapons Range. The Greenpeace campaign against the flight testing of cruise missiles had piqued the interest of the media in Canada; there was no doubt that media interest would spill over to the United States.

We did not yet know exactly when the test would occur, either. We did know that the U.S. military were obliged, by Transport Canada regulations, to issue a 48-hour advance 'Notice to Airmen' advising of the route, the time of departure, and the estimated duration of the flight. What we found out was, this information was made available to airline pilots, and was posted on the bulletin board in the pilot's lounge. We made the necessary contacts.

I was at home on Denman Island when I received the phone call: the cruise would be flying on Tuesday, February 19th.

We had worked out a detailed strategy for the action. The net was to be erected straddling the exact point in the road indicated by triangulation of data obtained from the cruise finding instruments. The rented van would be driven to Edmonton on Sunday evening. The campaigners would overnight there, and spend Monday the 18th getting the bottles of helium gas, and putting everything at the ready for the early Tuesday morning dash north.

Media relations, with emphasis on U.S. media, was my job.

The official line was that Greenpeace was going to loft a large net directly in the path of an unarmed cruise missile flying at a speed of 500 miles per hour at an altitude of 100 feet above the ground. The objective was to cause the missile's monitors onboard a nearby AWACS (Airborne Warning and Control Systems) aircraft to override the missiles programmed guidance system and manually alter the flight path of the cruise to avoid its being caught in the net. We were confident that such an interference would substantially defeat an important component of the test's objectives.

I spent Monday on the telephone, contacting the major TV media in the United States and Canada. On cruise-day, Tuesday the 19th, the Greenpeace team set up the net. On the previous Sunday, we had filed the required flight plan with Transport Canada, advising the time and place where we would loft the balloon-supported net. The net was tethered to a fence alongside the highway. About two hours before the cruise was expected, the media arrived—by helicopter and van. It was quite a scene. There, in the middle of a frozen Alberta tundra, representatives from ABC, CBS, NBC, ITV, and Japan TV, gathered.

Videographers, grudgingly, unpacked their equipment, for they were unanimous in the belief that there was no way Greenpeace could predict precisely where the cruise would cross the road.

Then, a loud noise directly overhead; the missile past exactly where Greenpeace predicted! But the altitude, at the point of crossing, was 1,000 feet, not the 100 feet programmed into the missile's guidance system. The military were taking no chances of the cruise being netted out of the air.

In Vancouver, we met at the Greenpeace office for a final media debriefing. I had copies of the first flight test video, and distributed them to the media representatives. That evening, the video was shown on newscasts all over the world.

The military claimed that our attempt to interfere with the cruise test had failed. That the test was a complete success. Doubts about their claim arose when they deferred the next test for three consecutive days, blaming inclement weather. But could it be that the cruise only flew accurately on clear, sunny days? Soon thereafter, the U.S. military announced that there would be no more cruise tests for the rest of 1985.

The cruise issue cooled somewhat in subsequent years for two principal reasons. The first was that NATO downplayed the cruise's importance *vis-a-vis* the Soviet led Warsaw Pact opposition. The second reason was the Gorbachev factor, which saw a relaxation in the nuclear war scenario concluding with the tearing down of the Berlin Wall in 1989. The cruise, as an air-launched and ground-launched weapon, lost much of its strategic value. It remained for the U.S. Navy to adopt cruise missiles as an important part of their attack system. They were deployed extensively during the Gulf War as a ship-launched weapon against land based targets.

You Can't Sink a Rainbow

Greenpeace, under the leadership of David McTaggart, went international in 1980. The ensuing process compelled the far flung Greenpeace offices to officially represent themselves at Council meetings which determined the budgetary allocations and campaign decisions. Patrick Moore, the former head of Greenpeace, before it was internationalized, was on the Board of Directors of Greenpeace International. It was predictable that McTaggart and Moore would eventually come to loggerheads over policy and campaign matters. Peter Bahouth, the USA international representative, brought unrelenting pressure on Moore to get him to resign his position on the Greenpeace International Board. Moore was deeply hurt by the accusations directed towards him; I sprang to his defense. The Greenpeace International Regional Director's meeting was held in Auckland, New Zealand, during the first days of July 1985. Moore and I were the North American regional representatives, and we traveled together to Auckland for the regional meeting. We discussed the move to displace him. I attempted to persuade Patrick that it was time to move on and avoid the terrible waste of energy that would be expended if he stubbornly fought to maintain his position on the International Board.

On arrival at Auckland, Pat and I went directly to the Greenpeace flagship, *Rainbow Warrior*, which was docked at Marsden wharf in downtown Auckland. The Captain, Pete Willcox, and International Executive Director Steve Sawyer, took us on a tour of the ship. It had just returned from relocating native people who were being subjected to unacceptably high levels of radioactivity from previous nuclear bomb tests near their island homeland of Rongelap. After the tour, we joined in with the crew for a toast to Steve on his 29th birthday.

As it was getting late, Patrick and I, and Mike Bossley from Australia drove out to the Piha Surf Club, where the meeting of Greenpeace Directors was to be held the following day. A bit later, Sawyer arrived at the Club. Unknown to us, at 11:38 p.m., just as we were getting ready to turn in, the *Rainbow Warrior* had been blown up. One person was killed: photographer Fernando Pereira was caught below decks by a second blast while attempting to salvage his camera equipment. The rest of the crew had made it to safety. It was later confirmed that the French Secret Service was responsible for the sinking.

The tragic consequence of Fernando's death and the sinking of the *Rainbow Warrior* pushed Greenpeace nuclear campaign activities to the top of the action agenda; the sinking, by the French, was seen as an act calculated to halt Greenpeace campaigns against their Government's testing of nuclear bombs on Moruroa Atoll.

Chernobyl

As if to punctuate the importance of nuclear issues, the tragedy of Chernobyl, in the Ukraine, unfolded. There, on April 26, 1986, a miscalculation by the reactors operators caused one of the electric power reactors at the site to go critical and explode. Thirty-one people died, 500 more were severely affected by the intense radioactive activity at the scene of the explosion and adjacent to it. Poisonous radioactive particles were carried by the wind, covering enormous areas of inhabited land between Kiev and the far north of Sweden, home of the Samit people who depend upon the caribou for their main source of food and income. Thousands of caribou had to be destroyed; their diet of mosses and lichens were contaminated by radioactive fallout, which, in turn, bio-accumulate in the animal's flesh, turning milk and meat unsafe. Radioactive fallout spread to Kiev, population of 2.5 million. Thousands of acres of farmland in the Ukraine were contaminated, and are still.

Since the young were more susceptible to radioactive poisons, Greenpeace came to the assistance of the Children of Chernobyl, recruiting, the world over, doctors and medical workers to volunteer their services.

The USSR Government refused to admit to the serious, and adverse, health risks caused by the Chernobyl accident. Blameless and defenseless, the people and animals of the affected nations looked forward to an uncertain future.

Global Environmental Governance

The Chernobyl incident illustrated the need for the creation of an appropriate venue for resolving trans-boundary issues. It seemed logical to expect that the United Nations would create a venue which would accommodate international problems such as that posed by the Chernobyl trans-boundary pollution issue. Unfortunately, the Untied Nations is structured in ways that guarantee protection of every nation's sovereignty. In plain language this means that all of the internal affairs of each nation are immune from interference by any other nation or group of nations. Many critics from outside the UN system had long objected to, and voiced their concerns about, the efficacy of world problem solving within the constraint of a nation's absolute sovereignty.

There are many issues today that fall into the category of trans-boundary events. The UN has strived to address them by creating voluntary agreements or treaties that may be subscribed to by individual nations. However, they are in no way compelled to comply. Exceptions to this situation are the decisions made by the Security Council, which are binding. For example, the economic sanctions against Iraq.

The shortcomings of the United Nations system are well documented, and are the concern of several Non Governmental Organizations (NGOs). The NGO which concentrates on United Nations charter reform, and global human rights, is the World Federalist Movement (WFM). They maintain a staffed office near to the United Nations buildings in New York City. The World Federalists of Canada (WFC) is one of several national offices of the WFM. The WFC office is in Ottawa, the nations capital.

At the time of joining the WFC, it was evident that this aware and concerned organization recognized the trans-boundary problems of air pollution, but had not campaigned very actively on that issue. The WFC concentrated on various aspects of human rights, and wasn't quite up to speed on global environmental issues. Recognizing this shortcoming, the WFC Council invited me in 1986, to join them as a nominee for a seat on Council.

After being elected, I introduced the notion that humans had the right to a clean environment, and that this component of human rights was more important than any other aspect: Of what value is the right to free speech in an atmosphere so polluted that one can no longer breathe the air or drink the water? Of all human rights, a safe environment is pre-eminent. The concept of elevating environmental concerns to the top of the global human rights agenda did not go down well with the old-guard of the World Federalist Movement. A sort of generational alignment prevailed. Many were charter members of the WFM since its origins in 1947. They had recognized the need for nations to relinquish some of their sovereignty in the interest of establishing a global governing structure that would serve to guarantee world peace. Caring for the environment as a vital part of the human rights agenda was not viewed as being sufficiently important to ask nation states to relinquish sovereignty. Some thought that introducing environmental protection to the human rights agenda would complicate and make the peace process more difficult. To their credit, the WFM gradually recognized the importance of a healthy environment and eventually became a major voice in demanding global governance over the planet's commons: the air, the sea, and outer space.

Members of the WFM number about 30,000 people in over 100 nations worldwide. Despite the relatively small membership, their dedication and focus on the issues, as well as their profound and credible analysis concerning them, has earned the WFC a high degree of respect among the United Nations community. My principal role on the Council was, and is, one of gadfly, in pursuit of promoting the environmental agenda.

Green Power

For the Greenpeace nuclear campaign, the sinking of the *Rainbow Warrior* and the Chernobyl nuclear power station disaster stimulated an enormous global response: membership increased from one million worldwide, in 1984, to more than three million. Greenpeace continued to grow, and it was clear that the organization had outgrown its founding location in Vancouver.

The logistics of Canada's enormous land mass and scattered population was a familiar problem to organizations attempting to go national. From a membership point of view, the population of British Columbia had already been saturated with Greenpeace fund-raising efforts. There was some fear that this basic support from the West would evaporate if Greenpeace were to move its administrative center to Toronto. Fortunately, the ground swell of citizens support of the environmental movement contributed to a surge of interest in British

Columbia as well as in Ontario. This unprecedented growth saw Greenpeace Vancouver expand into larger offices and engage in a broader range of campaign activity.

My day to day involvement in the administrative affairs drew to a close when the Board decided to appoint an Executive Director to run Greenpeace Canada. I reluctantly agreed, my hesitancy due principally to my personal dislike of centralized management. But I had to admit, that in this heady era of rapid expansion, there had to be some *one* organizing body to coordinate national administrative affairs to keep the growth express on track.

I remained on the Board of Directors, but had no other involvement in the management of Greenpeace affairs. Greenpeace International was engaged in the process of becoming 'solution oriented.' As a first step a committee was struck to evolve a sustainable energy policy. I had done a lot of research on that subject while compiling the draft for a Global Green Constitution. I joined the Greenpeace energy group. As well, the notion of sustainable development was being promulgated by the United Nations as an outgrowth of the World Commission on Environment and Development's final report. I, and several other Greenpeace Canada Board Members, produced an in-depth discussion paper on various aspects of sustainable development.

The five years from 1987 to 1992, will probably go down in history as the most dynamic, and successful, for the entire environmental movement, as well as, for Greenpeace. Public information polls consistently placed concern for the environment at the top of the list; more than 70 percent of the public considered environmental protection to be more important than job creation.

In 1987, the Montreal Protocol to preserve the ozone layer and control greenhouse gas emissions was endorsed by virtually every nation in the world. This meant that humans were finally admitting that their activities were of such magnitude that their adverse effects had global implications. And further, that collectively, humanity was going to do something to reduce the ecological impact of their depredations. In 1988, the Conference on the Changing Atmosphere was held in Toronto. This was the first major international meeting which brought Government and scientist together to discuss action on climate change. There, Governments voluntarily pledged to cut carbon dioxide emissions by 20 percent by the year 2005. Also noted during that conference, was that undeveloped nations contributed very little to these global problems, and consequently it should be the wealthy industrial nations that took the necessary action and paid the price for contamination. This position of the non-industrial nations awakened the world to the fact that the main instrument of well-being was economic growth, and that such growth contributes significantly to pollution and resource depletion. This observation gave rise to the notion that the industrialized nations had to double cut their emissions: one cut involved their own polluting output, and another cut to permit the still developing nations to increase pollution in their efforts to achieve economic growth. In concrete terms, this meant that the industrial world would have to cut greenhouse gas emissions by up to 80 percent by the year 2020. Although possible in theory, it was deemed impractical to achieve this reduction in polluting effects. Somehow a *quid pro quo* had to be reached.

After some time, the developed nations, mainly those belonging to the OECD (Organization for Economic Cooperation and Development), agreed to introduce non-polluting technologies to the developing world, so that they could grow economically without contributing much to global pollution. Although this was a logical solution, it did not prove to be politically feasible; no nation wanted to undermine its perceived economic structure by contributing to a potential competitor's industrial process. This was manifested by less and less funding for developing nations being approved by the various parliaments and legislatures of the so-called developed nations. Only Norway, Germany and Denmark responded by increasing their foreign economic aid.

1988 Federal Election

The 1988 Federal election was called on October 1; election day scheduled for November 21st. Concern about the environment had become number one, nationwide, in poll after poll. The Green Party intended to run candidates in at least the minimum required 50 electoral districts (out of the approximately 300 nationwide). I wasn't particularly interested in standing for election, for my wife and I had booked non-refundable flights for an extended, and long overdue, visit to her son at his home in Arizona.

The Green Party did not have a local constituency office, and due to my involvement with Greenpeace in Toronto and Vancouver, I did not have the time to do any local organizing. Consequently, we had a small membership, and had developed no process, nor carried on much of a search, for a suitable candidate. As well, the election had been called rather abruptly, which did not give us much time to prepare an effective campaign team.

As the registration date deadline approached, it looked as though the Greens might not field the necessary minimum of candidates, nationally. Reluctantly, and with some trepidation, I put my name forward and entered the contest. I learned, from standing for Parliament in the 1984 general election, that the media can serve as an asset to the cause of one's political position. By regularly issuing press releases, media representatives will cooperate in turn. One of the benefits of standing for election is that most newspapers will pay attention to your candidacy. It's free advertising for the party. Media people usually cooperate in the interest of fair coverage and the democratic right of all candidates to be heard.

With modern telecommunications equipment, such as fax, e-mail, and more recently Internet on-line services, it is affordable for even the poorest of political parties to put forth their arguments to a wide audience. Press releases can be sent at a keystroke. During election periods, thousands of people, their interest piqued by a touch of election fever, are offered alternatives which they otherwise would probably never hear, or for that matter read, in the daily press in between elections. On that score alone, it was worthwhile to expend whatever energy it took to conduct at least an information campaign. It was also important to enter a face-to-face debate with other candidates, should the opportunity present itself.

With few resources, I undertook to campaign in my home electoral district of Comox/Alberni, a geographic area of 1,000 square miles, much of the landscape mountains and ice. The major population centers, about 80 percent of the electorate, were concentrated in three communities, 30 miles apart, forming an approximate triangle. My campaign manager, and official agent, was Neil Horner, a volunteer from Vancouver. He was not available in the early stages of the campaign, so it was left to me to arrange for the making of election signs and to place them at strategic locations. A local artist made up twenty Green Party signs on sheets of plywood, and we drove to the urban areas and placed them in locations where they would be hard to ignore by passing motorists. My efforts were confined to preparing daily news releases for the local print and various electronic media. As well, I attended most of the all-candidates meetings.

Face-to-face conversations with individual voters was helpful in that I was able to determine their concerns and priorities. Most people were solidly in favor of Green Party policies, but, as before I was confronted with the same old attitude: no one wanted to waste their vote on a political party that had no chance of being elected.

CHAPTER 5

AS IF SURVIVAL MATTERS

1989 marked a watershed in global politics which had enormous implications for the environmental movement. The first dramatic event was the pulling down of the Berlin Wall, long a symbol of East/West confrontation. The second was the break up of the Soviet Union. This double blow to the solar plexus of the traditional Left was lauded by the Right as a victory of 'free enterprise' capitalism over 'progressive' socialism. As well, it soon became evident that the Soviet system had wreaked havoc on the environment and the health of its people to a much greater extent than had capitalist democracies.

The environmental movement was caught in an apparent contradiction. By inference, the capitalist system was the better protector of the environment. Therefore, capitalism was good not only for the economy, but also for the environment. The Right picked up on this 'fringe benefit' and used it to discredit environmental groups at a time when support from the progressive public was increasingly needed to halt the onrush of resource exploitation. The 1990s were to see the depletion of the protective upper atmosphere ozone layer, decimation of the world's fisheries, the destruction of the tropical and temperate rainforests, and an unwillingness to adhere to the global Climate Change Convention.

The organized Right was successful in that public support for environmental groups declined sharply in North America from the high point reached in 1989. Greenpeace was not affected much by loss of support, mainly due to its funding base in the European countries; the Euro-Nations maintain strong links to social democracy, which is basically capitalism with a human face. It is mainly the United States that puts forward its free enterprise agenda, and cornucopia concept, of a world awaiting the unleashing of its unlimited resources for, what turns out to be for the enormous benefit of the very few and to the detriment of everybody else.

It was also hard times for the Green political movement. The setbacks, however, served to weed out the less committed and saw the most dedicated rise to the leadership of the various Green Parties. The Greens persisted in organizing everywhere. They began to build more and more electoral support as people in many nations began to see that the capitalist agenda, dominant since the fall of the Berlin Wall, was exploiting the natural environment with an increasing frenzy and exhibiting little care in preserving the integrity of ecosystems.

The Greengrass Institute

Aware of obstacles to the achievement of electoral success, yet convinced of the necessity for Greens to contest elections at every level of government, I searched for a means that would enhance the credibility of the Green Party locally and globally: hence the founding of the Greengrass Institute in 1989.

The name evolved from consideration of where and how the institute would function. The 'Green' is obvious; the 'grass' is an acronym denoting that participants are Globally Responsible Advocates for a Sustainable Society. Since the various 'advocates' lived in far distant climes, we decided to communicate *via* e-mail.

The Institute was organized to stimulate a flow of ideas among various progressive thinkers drawn from a range of scholarly disciplines.

First, was the need to develop economic policy alternatives; second, to build a community of Green Parties that might be interested in forming a Green International, which would adhere to the basic components of a constitutional document that contained common global interests.

United Nations Conference on Environment and Development

The vehicle for launching this initiative was the upcoming United Nations Conference on Environment and Development. UNCED was to take place in Rio de Janeiro during June of 1992. In 1983, the World Commission on Environment and Development, under the leadership of Gro Harrlem Brundtland, Prime Minister of Norway, had produced a book entitled *Our Common Future*. It was a compendium of public opinion garnered from meetings held in many developed and underdeveloped nations. The essence of the deliberations was a clear message from the undeveloped South to the developed North: there could never be protection of the environment unless the South achieved a reasonable level of economic development.

The consequences of this conclusion were enormous. In an effort at expressing the situation, the term 'sustainable development' was introduced. The concept was accepted in principle by Government, by industry, and by a significant number of environmental organizations. 'Sustainable' remained open to whatever interpretation one cared to give it. As for 'development,' most defined it as economic growth. Obviously, it is not possible to sustain economic growth forever. The term promoted a debate among those interested and involved in the issue, posing more questions than solutions, and tending to split the environmental community.

Down Came the Berlin Wall

In 1989, the Berlin Wall was torn down. Shortly thereafter the USSR collapsed and began a reformation based on capitalist economic principles and democratic political processes. It was soon revealed that the Warsaw Pact nations and the USSR were grossly polluted. Health of whole populations was decreasing. In the former USSR deaths were exceeding births. Virtually no provisions were in place to contain and render most industrial wastes harmless. The adverse health effects grew so desperate that Soviet society was experiencing a reduction in the life span of their human population.

China, while adhering to a framework of communist ideology, rapidly adopted capitalist economic techniques and entered the global marketplace with great success. Ascendancy of capitalist economics accompanied by a thin patina of environmental greenwash rapidly dominated the debate.

Resource exploitation reached new highs, as demonstrated by the rapid growth of the logging industry in Canada, the United States and Russia. Brazil and other forested nations were clearing and burning their forests to pasture their livestock. Industrial activity everywhere was producing more greenhouse gasses. Combined with the rapid reduction of the global forest cover, the natural ability of the forested lands to absorb greenhouse gas emissions was reduced. To many the natural world was in dire straits.

To further illustrate the effects of rapid resource depletion, the world's great fisheries were declining. The cod fishery located on the Grand Banks of Newfoundland went extinct. Unemployment in the Maritime provinces of Canada soared. The Federal Government had to intervene with enormous financial subsidies to prevent entire communities from going bankrupt.

Over-fishing did not occur as an overnight phenomenon. For many years fisheries scientists warned about the probability of the cod fishery going extinct. To no avail. The North Atlantic Ocean was a part of the global commons; every nation fished it hard with evermore larger fish-boats and more sophisticated catching gear. For this situation there was no international agency that had sufficient clout to compel a reduction in the total catch.

In view of these hard facts, and faced with what I saw as a fast track to depletion of the planet with no effective opposition, I came to a difficult conclusion. The world had outgrown the system of sovereign states. A burgeoning global population, bent on achieving a living standard approaching that of the United States, was sucking the world dry of its vital essences that required thousands of millennia to accumulate. The ability of the Earth to support a sustainable future was thrown into question. The present system of governance was impotent to prevent global chaos brought on by resource depletion, and virtually no movement towards a political solution was in sight.

In 1989, the United Nations announced that the second world conference on environment and development would occur in Rio de Janeiro from June 1st to June 12th of 1992. The first UNCED (United Nations Conference on Environment and Development) had been held in Stockholm in 1972. It was there that the NGO community was 'allowed' to hold a parallel conference somewhat adjacent to the host hotel location. In the parking lot next to the hotel the Non Government Organizations from all over the world set up their displays and literature tables. Very little of the NGO input was acknowledged by the world's press, however, their presence was noted by the conference planners and their concerns and dedication played a large part in the planning of the 1992 UNCED event in Rio.

We, at the Greengrass Institute, were planning to attend the various preparatory conferences around the world that were build-ups to arriving at an agreed agenda. It soon became evident that most of the developed nations were dominating the deliberations. Their overarching presence resulted in reducing the impact of each agenda item. For instance, they reached an agreement, among themselves, that any substantive measures to protect the environment would not mandate compulsory compliance.

This measure reduced the effectiveness of addressing the conference issues, in a meaningful manner, to zero. NGOs, which fought valiantly to be given a say in the creation of the agenda, were dissuaded. They were allowed to attend the deliberations, but not to speak while in session. They could only act by buttonholing delegates at the lunch and coffee breaks, and perhaps at the toilets and urinals.

For this reason, we decided not to attend the formal proceedings. Instead we opted to participate in the alternate UNCED conference, the Global Forum, which was open to any NGO, approved or not, to voice their opinions. The venue for these 'unofficial' deliberations was Flamengo Park, a large ocean front facility near the center of Rio. The official UNCED meeting was held at a location fifteen miles outside of Rio, sequestered from the public. This arrangement made it very difficult for the many attendees who wanted to be involved in both the official and the unofficial conferences.

We, at Greengrass, set our own agenda. The document, which I had written in 1985 calling for a Global Green Constitution, was updated to 1989-90 and was distributed to every member of the official UNCED preparatory conference in April 1991. The document called for the approval and adoption of a protocol statement that would call for a system of global environmental governance.

The Brazil Protocol Towards a Global Green Constitution

The agenda for the 1992 United Nations Conference on Environment and Development (UNCED) was being prepared. The environmentalist community, supported by a rapidly growing public opinion, expected political commitment from the nation-states represented at the conference. There was a great deal of evidence which demonstrated that where no 'level playing field' existed, individual nation-states had little incentive to voluntarily implement the measures required to significantly reduce their contribution to global environmentally destructive practices.

It was suggested that a document, named the 'Brazil Protocol,' be offered for signature by member nations at ECO'92. A majority of UN member nations signatures would begin a process towards adoption of a Global Green Constitution. The Constitution would empower the United

Nations Security Council to impose sanctions against nation-states that refuse to comply with various Laws and Conventions which presently exist and undoubtedly would emerge from the 'Earth Charter' and 'Agenda 21' deliberations.

Paths To Green Governance		
	United Nations UNCED 1992	
Earth Charter		Brazil Protocol
Agenda 21		Global Green Constitution
	Green Governance	

Towards a Global Green Constitution: A Proposal

We are living in an historical period when it is questionable whether the human species will survive for much longer. We are being put at risk by a mistaken belief that Planet Earth has limitless resources and that humans are preordained to make use of them as rapidly as possible. We began the process in earnest at about the mid-point of the last century.

The industrial revolution reached its height during the mid 1960s. This fact, however, was only recognized during the 1970s when it became evident that global reserves of oil, the fuel that powers the engine of industrialization, had peaked.

During the 1980s another reality became evident: the entire planet's air, water, and land were being despoiled by human activity. So desperate is the situation that even the most conservative estimates indicate that unless we are able to fundamentally reverse this course by the end of this century, it is doubtful that life on this planet will survive.

The Problem

The ecologically malignant practices are deeply entrenched. They are virtually woven into the fabric of the prevailing human culture. It will require considerable time to adopt new cultural perspectives and a material infrastructure that will enable us to switch from an unsustainable present to a sustainable future. In view of these circumstances, the 1990s must become the decade of transition where the people of Planet Earth either join in the struggle for survival, or by doing nothing, opt for a gradual and excruciatingly painful descent towards oblivion. A planet-wide Sudan comes to mind. It would be naive to believe that the economic interests, with heavy investments in the business of converting the planet's resources as rapidly as possible and at the least cost, will voluntarily, or unilaterally, alter their ways in the interest of planetary survival. It will require an aroused citizenry imbued with what amounts to revolutionary fervor and stamina to turn around the existing mammoth commitment to unsustainable practices.

Global and Local Action

We are often urged to, 'Act Locally and Think Globally.' This phrase is not appropriate to global needs. Acting locally is vitally important, but it often leads to an illusion of accomplishment while the problems are transferred elsewhere. Thinking globally is only a prerequisite to the desperate need for acting globally. For example, in the context of one's community a victory may be achieved and citizens exultant in that they ran out of town the proposers for a toxic waste facility. However, this successful opposition often leads the proposers to search elsewhere in areas where few people in poor economic circumstances live. It may lead to illegal dumping where none can see it (like mixing the toxic waste with gasoline, to be burned by unsuspecting motorists in their cars) or by shipping the toxic wastes to other nations desperate for cash income.

National Nimbyism (the 'not in my backyard' syndrome), also occurs. There was the recent case where the Government of Canada shipped unwanted toxic chemical wastes to Britain. In this instance they were intercepted and returned to Canada. There is also the tragi-comedy of the garbage barge that no local or national entity wanted. Consequently, it began a voyage of aimless drift about the oceans, like the fabled Flying Dutchman, before the culprits finally undertook to responsibly deal with their own creation.

There is a clear need for global initiatives that aim to solve global problems. There are a variety of conventions among nations that work well. Across border mail, banking, and air traffic control are single issue functions upon which international agreements appear to operate smoothly. It is different as concerns the complex economic and social issues that affect the environment. The environment, however, cannot be considered in the context of single issues. A more comprehensive trans-national and socio-economic scope is required.

The unworkability of conventions concerning environmental protection is exemplified by the all important issue of carbon emissions as they contribute to the greenhouse effect, ozone depletion, and acid rain. The 1988 International Conference on the Atmosphere in Toronto illustrates this point.

The public was made to feel comfortable by an agreement that a 20 percent reduction in carbon would be achieved by the year 2005. Several well-known environmental groups accepted the 20 percent solution. What was not addressed is that while the developed nations would have achieved a 20 percent reduction, the less developed nations will have increased their carbon emissions to a point that would lead to a net global increase, even if the 20 percent reduction were achieved. The real numbers call for at least a 50 percent reduction of carbon by the developed nations, by 2005, and 70 percent by 2020, when the world population of humans is projected to reach the 10-billion mark.

It remains doubtful whether even the first 20 percent reduction will occur. The Canadian Government on several occasions has raised doubts about Canada's achieving the target on the grounds that doing so would make the nation uncompetitive in the global marketplace. The United States Government will only agree to stabilizing greenhouse gasses by 2005. Since carbon is only one of the contributors to climate change, the U.S. decision will result in a global carbon increase from sources that already contribute 30 percent of the global total. It is worth noting that Denmark, Germany, and Sweden have agreed to reduce carbon emissions by the 20 percent target figure by the year 2005.

Global Politics

Problems—such as the greenhouse effect, holes in the ozone layer, trans-boundary effects of toxic pollution on the quality of air, water, soil—transcend narrow national political interests. It is evident that elimination of existing and proposed dangerous technologies cannot be resolved by appeals that depend upon unilateral action. Apart from ethical considerations, there is little obligation for nations to accept their share of the cost of cleaning up the planet. Governments will continue to employ the excuse that they cannot compete with nations that continue to produce with few environmental protection measures in place.

In view of the refusal to comply with scientifically derived and convention agreed to limits, there is a clear need to develop a global political agenda that will mandate enforcement of international agreements. *A level playing field* must be established on a global basis. Either every nation state opts to do its proportionate share in maintaining the quality of the global environment, or none will have much of an incentive to do it unilaterally.

Revolutionary Fervor

The revolution to achieve planetary survival—and we are involved in that revolution right now—is far more all-encompassing and profound than to become involved in an armed struggle. We don't take up arms against those responsible for the desertification of North Africa which has caused the death of millions and removed habitat which presaged the elimination of other creatures with whom we share this Earth. For how can one wage war on cattle, or the doctors and nurses, long dead as well, who risked life and limb to bring medicine and public health measures to the people, thus precipitating a huge population increase in Africa where a delicate ecological balance is easily upset.

This revolution has different imperatives. It is the struggle against time. It needs to be non-violent. It stems from a realization that humans have altered the face of this Earth so profoundly that unless prompt action is taken we are all doomed. This revolution is against the prevailing cultural attitudes that have caused the despoliation: as well, against the institutions of church, state, and business that resist fundamental change.

We need to bring about a global 'perestroika' based on the fundamental precept that humans no longer have to live in fear of nature. Everything depends upon how well we care for Planet Earth and one another. This leads to a basic commitment: Sustainability with Social Justice. To survive we need to learn a different way of thinking: holistic, non-linear, comprehensive. All terms that describe an interrelationship of issues, which taken individually, stand analytically independent. It is a recognition of their interdependence which describes the whole. This new way of thinking leads to a more accurate perception of complex processes such as the human body, atomic physics, and the politics of survival.

The issues to be considered in a politically comprehensive manner are: Social Justice; Economic Equality; Environmental Protection; Disarmament. It is just co-incidental that the first letter of the four issues results in the acronym, SEED, but this acronym may yet prove prophetic.

Social Justice

Human Rights: Green governments will oppose any culture if it proves to be prejudicial by reasons of gender, age, color, race, religion, belief, sexual orientation, mental or physical condition, marital status, family composition, source of income, political belief, nationality, language preference, place of origin. There are a host of social justice movements today, mostly in the developed nations. Women are struggling to achieve equal pay for work of equal value, and legal control over their own bodies. Prevailing patriarchal attitudes are sanctioned, or most often studiously ignored, and least often grudgingly modified. These intolerable attitudes often result in physical and emotional abuse to women, children, and gays.

Cultural Imperatives: Some nation-states are institutionally prejudiced against minorities: Native Indians, Jews, Blacks, East Indians, etc. Although cultural imperatives are deeply entrenched and often transcend 'reason' they must be accepted as realities complete with warts. However, all cultures need to modify their precepts when threatened from without, or they become extinct. Historically, cultures become extinct when they don't modify in time; ignorance of change about to occur, simply overtakes intransigent cultures. In view of this historical precedent, cultural modification needs to be preceded by education. Today, we have the means to educate masses of people by a variety of ways. When looking for an example of cultural modification through 'education,' blue jeans and rock music are examples that come to mind. A green government will persist in educating people about the need for basic human rights among which is the aforementioned prejudicial treatment of minorities.

Economic Equality

Global Economic Equality: The principle of global economic equality is central to a green government's population policy. The cornerstone of economic equality is an assured basic income from birth to death for every woman, man, and child on Earth. Free medical and dental care, education to the highest level of a person's interest and capability, and most importantly, access to socially useful work.

Economic equality at the needs level for all would help to reduce tensions that lead to war. It would establish the economic security that is a major factor in achieving a steady-state human population. It would help to enshrine human rights. It would stimulate initiative in the arts, commerce, technological innovation, small-scale enterprise in general and non-exploitive home industry. It would acknowledge the economic value of non-salaried work in the home, community, and volunteer organizations. It would enable homesteaders and farmers to afford the practice of sustainable agriculture. It would encourage cooperation rather than competition. It would tend to limit the drift of people from the country to urban areas, especially in developing nations.

Demographic Transition: One of the more basic actions that green governments must take towards the establishment of policies that lead to economic security concerns human population. How many humans can this region support? What is the relationship between human population in this region and the rest of the world? These questions are central to any globally relevant commitment. Where do we begin to look for guidelines that will ultimately define the parameters by which decisions concerning population may be taken? If we accept the reality that people cannot be ordered to limit their numbers, they will have to do so voluntarily. Empirical studies show that in nations where women are well educated, and where the people are reasonably economically secure, their population tends to stabilize at replacement levels. In some instances, as in parts of Europe, the numbers of people are actually declining. It is worth noting that this decline occurs despite government policy which often gives incentives to have more children.

Carrying Capacity: It is almost axiomatic to any study of population and material resources that there must be some limits as to what Planet Earth can sustainably yield. That limit is known as carrying capacity. Consequently, it is incumbent upon each Government to determine the carrying capacity of the region under their governance. Population policy would flow from carrying capacity according to a formula that would include addressing basic human needs to effect the demographic transition while preserving the habitat of native flora and fauna. Central to the policy would be a commitment from the more developed nations that have already effected the demographic transition to assist others less fortunate.

Energy Accounting: Perhaps the most demonstrative way to illustrate the availability of resources is the measure of energy required to make them available. The mining of copper can serve as an example. Several hundred years ago copper was found in a pure state in surface outcropping. A few blows with a hammer would release this valuable material, ready to use. Now, copper has to be mined from deep in the Earth and smelted from rock that yields up about 1 percent of its volume of pure metal. The ore crushing and smelting process consumes large quantities of energy and the leftover waste materials are laden with trace quantities of toxic metals that will ultimately leach into streams and rivers. This illustrates that the limits to copper's availability are not defined by the amount of the resource, *per se*, but the energy required to produce it and the environmental impact of the whole process. When we resolve the issue of resource use to the energy required to extract them, we then need to look at energy supply. Despite an heroic science that ranges from the illusory 'fusion in a test tube' to grandiose schemes of harnessing energy released in a hydrogen bomb explosion, the reality emerges that we are dependent for 80 percent of our total energy from the combustion of fossil fuels: coal, oil, and natural gas. And, it is mostly the combustion process that is responsible for creating the greenhouse effect, acid rain, and ozone layer depletion.

A Green Energy Policy: A green government's energy policy would choose only those processes that are safe, renewable, ecologically benign and equitably available to everyone on a global basis. Those energy sources are direct solar, wind, wave, tidal, small-scale hydro, biomass, and perhaps geothermal. There are many studies to determine limits to the global availability of safe, renewable energy sources. A consensus among analysts seems to be about 12 billion kilowatts (KW) or more conveniently, 12 Terawatts (TW).

This means that it is feasible to produce 12 TW of energy continuously without significantly disrupting ecosystems or incurring the further diminution of wildlife species or their habitat. At present global population levels it would mean that each person could employ about 2 KW, assuming equal allocation of energy. To put these numbers into perspective, the economically developed nations would consume 7.5 KW of energy per person; the less developed nations, 1.1 KW. The difference in material lifestyles between these two sectors is approximately the difference in energy use. Total global energy use is currently 13.5 TW—more than could be supplied by safe renewable sources of energy. These numbers are a sure indicator of why we must address the question of sustainability and more equitable distribution now, before the options run out for a peaceful transition to a just and sustainable global society.

Doing More With Less: Numerous studies indicate that up to 50 percent of present day energy use is wasted. Energy efficiency would provide the same level of goods and services that are presently available. Some researchers conclude that about 1 KW of energy, *per capita*, used efficiently, would effect the demographic transition to a point where global population would stabilize at about 10 billion. This is approximately twice present world population. If we accept the estimate of 12 available from safe renewable sources of energy, then 1.2 KW would be assured for everyone, forever. To visualize a global society safely living at the material level of assured basic needs, is possible.

Obviously, the exact quantity of energy consumed, *per capita*, would not be uniform everywhere. Regional climate differences and distances between population centers would considerably alter the equity equation. However, accommodating these differences would still yield equal amenity value for everyone.

If More Is Better: Estimates indicate that 3 KW per person, employed efficiently, could deliver a material lifestyle that would approximate the present level of amenity 'enjoyed' by the developed nations. If global equity were practiced where everyone had access to the benefits of a 3 KW 'allocation' then the global population would have to be reduced to 4 billion from the present 5.2 billion and the anticipated steady-state of 10 billion persons. The demographics of this population scenario suggests a global policy, for an undetermined period, of one child per family.

Environmental Protection

Resources: The crop-land upon which we are depending to feed a population that is expected to double over the next 30 years is rapidly vanishing. It is being eroded and blown away due to market and other economic pressures on farmers. Consequently, they are not able to practice sustainable agriculture.

Underground water presently being used for crop irrigation in the U.S. Southwest will be dried up within 25 years. Thousands of acres of crop-land are abandoned each year due to salination from unsustainable irrigation practices. This land cannot be renewed. The chlorinated fluro-carbons (CFC) used in spray cans, foamed insulation, and as in refrigerants, cause holes in the upper atmosphere ozone layer. That layer protects us against skin cancer caused by the harmful rays of the sun. If we cease to produce CFCs, we could no longer freeze food or keep beer cold. People that cannot afford to purchase refrigerators or freezers are subject to the same cancer causing factors as those who can afford them. Global equality already exists when it comes to sharing the effects of pollution.

In addition to depletion of non-renewable resources, we are using up potentially renewable resources faster than they can be replaced. (Trees and fish are principal examples.) Rather than develop income energy technologies by employing the sun, wind, water, and biomass, we continue to pump oil from the ground and increase dependence on unreliable supplies of imported oil because it is still relatively inexpensive. Despite the experience of Chernobyl, we continue to build and make plans for more and more nuclear power plants, instead of adopting policies of energy conservation.

Rather than produce goods that are long lived in the first instance, readily reparable, and recyclable, we continue to manufacture products for superficial style and questionable function, then spend billions of dollars manipulating the public into purchasing them.

This waste and inappropriate use of energy and resources would be addressed by green governments in the form of resource use taxes based upon life-cycle costing of the products made from them. By way of this regulatory process, the selling price of the product would have added to it the cost to society of resource use environmental impacts. Products having a long service life, that are simple to maintain, low in energy use, and readily recyclable would be less expensive. Such tax disincentives would initiate a transition to a sustainable society, and would make renewable sources of energy and recycling more economically attractive.

Wildlife: One cannot depend entirely upon a market driven economy to protect the planet. Some would pay any tax, for cost increases would not put ecologically inappropriate products out of reach for all customers. An example of this are the horns of African rhinos, and elephant tusks. These are 'products' socially valued by some cultures where no market price seems too high. Consequently, it is necessary to address the preservation of the global ecosystem that is composed of elements that must remain inviolate—exempt from human exploitation. For thousands of years humans have been eradicating whole species of animals and plants to accommodate human population increase. The great auk, the passenger pigeon, are both extinct. Many predators, especially wolves, coyotes, foxes, grizzly bears, eagles, have been virtually eliminated from former habitats. Present society will tolerate them in zoos, or in very small numbers in the wild, for when they marginally occupy human territory, or eat animals that are 'reserved' for humans, these predators are relentlessly searched out and destroyed. Then, when they appear to be on the verge of total extinction, collective guilt sometimes results in great efforts to preserve the few that remain.

Hundreds of thousands of dollars are being spent to preserve the California condor, where no mating pairs exist in the wild. And the bald eagle, the rare and endangered symbol of U.S. power, is gradually being reintroduced, and grudgingly accepted, into areas where they had previously been decimated by farmers, ranchers, and loss of habitat.

Green governments would recognize that the conflict between humans and wildlife will not disappear of itself. Wildlife must be protected by establishing protected habitats where human access is prohibited, except to apprehend the inevitable trespassers, poachers and vandals. There, in wilderness, wild animals and plants can live, undisturbed by human activities. There comes a time, according to some, that wild life will overpopulate their territory and populations will crash due to insufficient food. Consequently, human predators (read hunters) need to intervene to keep the balance. This is called wilderness resource management, an oxymoron, for if we simply set aside protected habitats of sufficient size, nature will 'regulate' her own as she has for millennia.

The Global Ecosystem: The Planet Earth as an ecosystem in, and of, itself was conceptualized by James Lovelock, a space scientist. He named it the Gaia hypothesis. It suggests that the Earth's temperature is closely regulated within necessarily narrow limits by growing plants. The planetary ecosystem, very simply, consists of the sun, plus moisture, that cause plants to grow. The plants absorb carbon dioxide from other biological activity and gives off oxygen which is taken in by other organisms. The process regulates the atmospheric moisture, which in turn controls the Earth's temperature. The hypothesis predicts global temperature changes if this balance is disturbed by large-scale intervention in the natural process.

Humans are causing that large scale intervention. The burning of fossil fuels increases the amount of carbon dioxide (among other pollutants) in the atmosphere. The rapid eradication of the tropical rainforests is depleting the Earth's plant growth and diminishing the capability for absorbing carbon dioxide. The unabsorbed carbon dioxide rises to the upper atmosphere and blocks the re-radiation of solar energy back into space. This precipitates a global temperature increase called the 'greenhouse effect,' which scientists predict will cause the ice caps to melt. This, in turn, will increase ocean levels causing inundation of coastal cities, valuable crop lands, and estuarian ecosystems all over the world. It will also cause increase of land temperatures, resulting in further shortfalls of fresh water to grow crops and will encourage the spread of deserts.

Restorative Measures: A green government would address these problems in the same way that a nation-state being attacked would normally respond. They would mobilize the best brains and spare no expense in an attempt to resolve the problems. Large scale transfer payments between nations may be necessary to provide incentives to preserve certain lands as wilderness to protect endangered ecosystems. For example, the Brazilians offer the same justification for cutting down their rainforests as Europeans and North Americans did for cutting down most of their forested land. The major 'benefit' from chopping down the forests was an increase in agricultural land on which to grow crops and pasture animals.

By applying techniques that we know now, it would have been possible for the Europeans and North Americans to cut trees off the best agricultural land and 'manage' the marginal lands for timber and forest cover so that the net effect would be no decrease in biomass from the 'original' tree cover. This is the recommended solution for Brazil and other affected tropical areas. It is in the interests of preserving global ecosystems to subsidize this activity.

Disarmament

The world spends $1,150 billion U.S. dollars a year on armaments. The money itself has little intrinsic value but it represents valuable and scarce resources used for no purpose other than putting one another to death.

The money spent represents the creative energy of some of the best brains in all nations of the world in the building, deployment, and use of these machines of death. Redirection of material and human resources could fund the required elements of a global sustainable society.

It would be naive to believe that war between, and within, nation-states is likely to disappear with the abolition of nuclear weapons. However, this fact does not imply that we can tolerate their existence. It is imperative that weapons-grade related nuclear technology be put back into Pandora's Box. This policy would lead to the end of nuclear power. The needed radioisotopes for medical use could be obtained from research reactors that do not have the capability for the production of plutonium, which is the necessary component for a nuclear bomb.

Construction of nuclear power facilities underway, or planned, would be halted and canceled. Presently operating power reactors would need to be shut down immediately. Those nations requiring a phase out period, due to unavoidable dependence on nuclear produced electricity, would be obliged to have their nuclear facilities placed under 'trusteeship' until the last nuclear power plant and its spent fuel was interred in an above ground concrete sarcophagus where an around-the-clock vigil would need to be kept for 40,000 years.

Eradication of nuclear technology is vital, but it is only a first step in the disarmament process. In the wings are a host of other weapons that are less dramatic but have a death dealing potential the equal of small nuclear weapons. Chemical, biological, deep penetrating explosive, long range pinpoint delivery systems add up to a devastating array of weaponry that most certainly will emerge as dominant when the threat of nuclear weapons no longer exists. The nuclear arms race squeezes even the most robust economies. Conventional warfare conducted with sophisticated weapons is no less expensive, as we have observed during the Gulf War.

The U.S. and the USSR, although militarily powerful, lost ground in the commercial world for reasons directly associated with their, up to now, fanatical persistence in out-gunning one another. Meanwhile, Japan and West Germany, losers in the last World War, forbidden to build weapons, applied their creative potential and resources to commerce. Without having to burden their economies with building weapons they have surpassed the U.S. and the USSR by conventional measures of economic performance.

Modern sophisticated weapons don't accomplish their objective to drive an opponent to its knees. They are ineffectual when used against people who want more than anything else to be free to choose their own way. This was demonstrated in Vietnam and Afghanistan. We have subtly entered the historical period where wars of aggression are un-winable in the face of a dedicated organized 'social' defense by less powerful nations who's people are prepared to sacrifice all to resist the oppressor.

Framing a Constitutional Document: An Overview

The debate has been prompted by evidence that life on this planet is in jeopardy. There is little doubt that a global politics is necessary. The question is how do we achieve binding agreements in law that are enforceable and would oblige each nation, regardless of size and wealth, to abide by them.

There would be need for an agency to prevent eco-vandals from acting unilaterally. An enforcement agency would need the power to act without being invited by the offending nation. We can probably anticipate that one or more nations will abrogate an agreement. Consequently, there must be effective and enforceable sanctions ready for application. This need not be a feared legislative measure, for once in place, nations considering violations would be deterred just from the 'knowing' that they will not be tolerated. Offenders would face collective opposition from the other nations. The principle is that no one nation would be more powerful than the coalition of nations that would oppose any abrogation of a Global Green Constitution.

Basic Objectives

A Global Green Constitution would represent a world-around political expression about a radical but necessary value system. It will reflect values that enshrine a sustainable society with social justice for all.

Its ratification would mean an end to national governments unilaterally exercising their present prerogatives of sovereignty. Instead, Governments would be elected to office that could most effectively formulate and institute national policy according to the tenets of a Global Green Constitution.

Role for the United Nations

It is logical for the United Nations to undertake responsibility for exercising Global Green Constitutional authority, but there may be some serious structural problems imposed by the UN Charter which need to be addressed. As presently constituted, the United Nations General Assembly has no enforcement powers. Decisions are made by the Security Council. The Council is composed of fifteen members. Five of these members are permanent. The other ten are elected for a two-year term by the General Assembly. Council decisions require nine affirmative votes. Each permanent Security Council member possesses what amounts to veto power over any Security Council decision. The five nations having this veto power are the USA, China, Russia, France and the United Kingdom. It would not be appropriate for these five, who collectively and separately are among the most prolific abusers of the global environment, to have veto power over decisions involving a Global Green Constitution.

There is an avenue of hope that the veto power of the permanent members can be negated. Article 27 of the UN Charter, states that:

> ...in decisions under Chapter VI and under paragraph 3 of Article
> 52, a party to a dispute shall abstain from voting.

From the perspective of being involved in coping with the global nature of the problems we are facing, only a Global Green Constitution that has international legal standing and the collective support required to enforce compliance will solve the most pressing of problems that affect global survival.

It is hoped that the analysis and suggestions for action presented in this essay will generate a SEED that will be sown about the globe and rooted everywhere.

UNCED: UN Conference on Environment and Development

By 1992, interest in the upcoming UNCED meeting was building to a fever pitch. Environmental protection was at the top of every national agenda. This interest resulted in 116 heads of nation states indicating that they were attending. In all, 172 nations were going to be represented at the Rio conference. This translated into 8,000 registered delegates and 9,000 members of the press. More than 3,000 NGOs received accreditation. UNCED was to be the largest conference in the history of the United Nations.

The choice of Rio de Janeiro was at first criticized due to the instability of its currency, corruption, street crime and roaming bands of self-appointed vigilantes rounding up, and even killing, street children. Brazil was a nation with the greatest disparity of income between the rich and the poor. It professed democracy, but practiced oligarchy. Brazil did not look to be an appropriate venue for a global meeting to enact an ecological preservation agenda inclusive of human rights.

Brazil had very little in the way of ecological protection measures. Vast areas of the enormously bio-productive rain forest was being torn down and burned to make way for cattle grazing: the flesh of the animals served up as hamburger makings in the MacDonalds' of the world. Though, on second thought, what better venue could be chosen to hold a world conference on human rights and protection of the environment than in the proverbial 'belly of the beast.'

The Road to Rio

I had built up a working relationship with an educational television broadcast station called the Knowledge Network. They had not budgeted to be present at Rio themselves, yet, they wanted to do a retrospective on UNCED in their Vancouver studios soon after our return. I was, therefore, contracted by Knowledge to do media work in Rio: principally, to secure stock footage from onsite producers. Nevertheless, this assignment gave me the opportunity to access the official media facilities of the formal conference, and the Forum, which proved to be of great value in promoting the issue of Global Environmental Governance—the main aim of the Greengrass Institute.

So, we, at Greengrass, began to plan the details of my expedition to Rio. Aside from finding the necessary finances, we had to establish contact with the Brazilian functionaries to secure a suitable venue for our presentations. After faxing and phoning back and forth, it was understood that the conference room at the Banco do Brasil, in downtown Rio, would be available for the Greengrass seminars on Global Environmental Governance. We worried about having our seminars take place further than walking distance from Flamengo Park, where most of the Forum action was to take place. We were assured that a tram service connecting all the venues would be provided to all Forum attendees, free of charge. Somewhat mollified, we accepted.

As for airline ticketing, I had attended many Greenpeace board meetings in Toronto. The frequent flyer points were accumulating; I hoped by June, I would have sufficient to fly to Rio and back, for free.

Hotel accommodation was another problem. In the first half of this century, Rio had been the 'in' holiday destination of people from all over the world. After World War II, as Brazil's governing structure eroded, corruption and street crime proliferated. Vacationers were molested, even murdered, on the beaches and seaside walkways and Rio gradually lost its allure. As tourism subsided, the hotels sank into senescence. Very few newer hotels were available, and I soon found them already fully booked by the entourages of the official delegations.

A friend told me that the Trocadero Hotel, fronting on the Copacabana Beach, was one of the finest of the old line accommodations.

A few phone calls to them, and after some negotiating I paid, in advance, in U.S. dollars, the full amount covering the two-week booking period. Fortunately, the sum was not extravagant: neither, though, were the hotel's accommodations.

The Canadian Government was promoting NGO participation at the Rio conference. They indicated a willingness to subsidize some of the travel expenses. We applied and obtained a small sum which would defray at least anticipated meal costs.

We printed 5,000 copies of a brochure, in poster format, advertising the seminars, with the intention of distributing them at information kiosks placed in various locations within the Global Forum.

The Brazil Greens were hosting a conference which called for Greens all over the world to attend. This conference was to precede the official opening of the UNCED, on June 1. I was appointed the official delegate of the Green Party of Canada. I looked upon this as a good omen, for I had for some years been advocating that a Green International was absolutely necessary for building a global sustainable society.

Flying Down to Rio

May 28, 1992, was a good day to fly. Marie drove me to the local airport at Comox, B.C., about fifteen miles north of Denman Island. I was booked on a regional flight which would connect with a trans-Canada flight from the Vancouver hub to Toronto. Then overnight, and twelve hours, non-stop to Rio, but this trip would not be uneventful.

Things went wrong even before taking off from Comox. The connector flight was delayed due to 'traffic control' problems in Vancouver. The Toronto connecting flight timing was 'tight.' This meant that my 50 pounds of brochures could not be offloaded from the connector flight to the Toronto airplane in time. But they might hold the Toronto flight for me. By the time the connector reached Vancouver, I found that my scheduled Toronto airplane had already left. My baggage meanwhile was loaded onto another flight, different from the next one on which there was space for me. For all I knew, my baggage, especially the valuable seminar notices, were on their way to the vast emptiness of the Canadian arctic, instead of Rio.

I arrived in Toronto, after a long milk-run flight that stopped at three Canadian cities. On the advice of an airline employee I went to the Lost Baggage Claim office, and there, in their somewhat tattered exterior were the two bundles of notices and my traveling bag. United once again, I was determined not to be separated from any part of my luggage.

I booked in to my host's house for a bit of sleep then made my way to Pearson airport to board the evening Canadian Airlines flight for the 6,000 mile, twelve hour, non-stop flight to Rio.

The airplane was mostly carrying attendees to the Rio UNCED conference. Among the passengers was the Honorable Jean Charest, Minister of the Environment, and his entourage. Sequestered in Business Class, we had little opportunity to speak with him. Charest had been under attack from the Canadian environmental movement to sign on to the upcoming Biodiversity Treaty and the Framework Treaty on Global Climate Change initiative.

Canada lacked an environmental protection act, and the Tories, who were governing the nation came up with a deceptive document named the Green Plan. It was supposed to be a far-reaching and definitive initiative that would solve all of Canada's environmental problems. The criticism from the environmental community was harsh. It was perhaps best expressed by Dan McDermott, the campaign coordinator for Greenpeace Canada. According to McDermott, the Government initiative was "neither green, nor a plan."

The flight to Rio from Toronto entered Brazilian airspace during the night. As we traversed that country's vast rainforest, it was possible to discern where Brazil's borders began by the line of the fires burning. Even from our 37,000 foot altitude the dark sky was illuminated by the endless pyres. We were witnessing the destruction of perhaps the most bio-diverse of the Earth's ecosystems; it was a terribly depressing sight.

At about 7:00a.m., on a clear May 30th, the jet landed at Rio's Galeao International Airport, but the aircraft did not dock at a regular airline space. Instead, the plane was parked on the edge of a minor landing strip away from the main arrivals terminal. There, we were met by several small buses. Blue clad uniformed young women guided the passengers aboard the vehicles. The buses then motored to an Customs and Immigration staging area. Here we were separated into three lines: registered UNCED conference attendees; those attending the Global Forum; and returning citizens.

I had to choose one of the lines; I had credentials which entitled me to enter either as a registered Global Forum participant, or as a press person for the Knowledge Network. I chose the Global Forum immigration entry, for I felt that there would be much more 'action' at the Forum than at the formal UNCED conference.

A flight attendant had advised during the flight to Rio to be aware of the criminals that hung around the airport promising a cheap ride to the various hotels, only to stop at some out of the way location in order to steal your money, your credit cards or other valuables. The crooks were so clever, pilots themselves, after several years of flying back and forth to Rio, had been mugged and relieved of their wallets. The attendant gave a short course in protecting oneself while in and around airport surface transportation.

This awareness made me anxious and tense. I chose a 'safe' hot and sweaty, supposedly air-conditioned, public bus to connect up with my hotel. I also found a 'buddy' who was going to the same hotel as me.

The bus trip into town passed through a cross section of slowly decaying Rio. Virtually every building we passed looked like a long abandoned industrial site: broken windows and trash wracked streets abounded. Eventually we emerged on the Atlantic Ocean Parkway, and some of the glories of Rio architecture became apparent. The Forum's check-in point, Hotel Gloria, was a wonderful example of 19th Century French neo-classical architecture.

After confirming my arrival, I hailed a 'safe' taxi and handed the driver a paper on which I had printed Hotel Trocadero. It turned out that there were two Trocaderos. He, of course, had taken me to the wrong one, the one located in the heart of the Rio red light district. The driver could speak no English, and I no Portuguese. Finally, I thought to mention Copacabana—Hotel Trocadero on the Copacabana Beach—and his eyes lit up in recognition.

At the hotel, I had to negotiate a room for the two days in advance of the date that my reservation was booked: the early arrival due to the pre-conference meeting of the Green Party International.

I reached my room, on the seventh floor, after a ride in a rickety, somewhat reluctant, elevator. It was equipped with an air conditioner which didn't cool, a small refrigerator which roared constantly, electric light switches that predated Edison, and a telephone connected to a wall outlet by bare copper wires. The one closet contained a small safe which could, presumably, be unlocked *only* by using the key given me when I checked in. The hotel clerk warned that it was important to my welfare that I wear no jewelry, even a cheap wristwatch, so as not to attract the attention of the hordes of pickpockets and thieves that thronged the streets and beaches.

Welcome to Rio de Janeiro!

I awakened early the next morning to go for a pre-breakfast walk on the beach. To my surprise there were two Khaki uniformed Uzi armed troopers lolling around the outside of the hotel entrance. One of the hotel employees called to me and warned that until the first day of the UNCED conference, when the whole Brazilian militia would be deployed in Rio to clean up the streets, that it wasn't a good idea for me to walk along Avenue Atlantico, to say nothing about strolling on the beach where I was almost certain to be assaulted.

Feeling a prisoner in my hotel room, I ate my meals in the hotel restaurant, and that evening I hired a private chauffeur-driven car to take me to the Green International conference hotel. On the way, juxtaposed behind the elaborate hotels along the beach, I noticed the *favellas*. The poorest of the poor lived in their windowless shacks, cheek by jowl, against the protective walls of multimillion dollar condos.

The Green International meeting was, to my gratification, well attended. Several Euro Parliamentarians were there. The conference was chaired by a Green from Brussels. Simultaneous translation service in six languages was available, although English appeared to be the language of choice by most of the participants. This mini Green United Nations was surprisingly together on its agenda. After only two days of meetings a consensed statement of principles was achieved.

Buoyed by this show of green solidarity and purpose, I faced the real world of Rio de Janeiro in a more optimistic frame of mind.

On arrival back at my room in the Trocadero Hotel I settled in for my second night in Rio. I attempted to phone home to say I had arrived okay. All the lines were busy, and upon inquiry at the desk I was told, 'just keep trying, in an hour or so you should be able to complete your call.' After some time I finally got through, and then washed up and climbed into bed just as the phone rang. It was the front desk. The management wanted me to settle up my bill for food, for the phone call, and for the first extra night. I questioned why I was being asked to pay up now, at one-o'clock in the morning. The clerk said that the next day currency was going to be devalued by 20 percent, and that they needed U.S. dollars now so they could make a bank deposit to avoid taking a loss. I reluctantly complied. Aside from my prepaid accommodation, virtually every day of my two week stay I settled my account with U.S. funds.

From my hotel window I had a partial view of startlingly white sand beach. Though crowded with people, almost no one was in the water. It is true that breakers created a strong undertow, but the real impediment was the pollution of the waters emanating from the *favellas* that abounded on the hillsides in back of the beach hotels and condos. Having no electricity, no garbage collection, nor sewage disposal, all wastes eventually found their way into the ocean.

I was gratified to learn that no building could be erected on the sea side of Avenue Atlantico which ran along the full length of the beach-side frontage. As well, there was a wide sidewalk and dedicated bicycle path which allowed pedestrians and cyclists to travel unimpeded by cross traffic for at least ten miles of Atlantic Ocean beach front. This accommodation for the ordinary people, in a land ruled by an oligarchy of the rich, was unexpected.

To my pleasant surprise, a film crew from the Vision Network out of Toronto was headquartered at my hotel, and we got together often to go out for supper as a group. Restaurant food found around the Copacabana area was sumptuous and cheap.

More or less acclimated to the muggy hot weather and the customs and cautions of Rio street life, I was ready to wend my way to Flamengo Park and partake in the official opening day ceremonies of the '92 Global Forum, so I loaded my backpack with Greengrass brochures and hailed a 'safe' taxi, in a rainy drizzle and rapidly rising temperature, and was driven to the Gloria Hotel.

I posted notices of the Greengrass seminar at the hotel and then crossed the temporary pedestrian-only bridge which spanned Avenue Atlantico and terminated at the entrance to Flamengo Park where the Global Forum was taking shape. Most of the exhibitions consisted of tent structures spaced along the multitude of paved walkways throughout the park. This arrangement, among tall palms and other mature tropical trees and greenery, was a pleasant alternative to the stark auditorium and parking lot venue of the formal UNCED deliberations. Rather quickly the Global Forum came to be a restful haven for many of the official UNCED delegates. It was an overwhelming sight. Imagine 25,000 people, from nations around the world, gathered to exchange ideas on what we, collectively, needed to do to construct a sustainable global society.

There was so much to see and do. It would require at least five people, each one every day attending concurrent sessions and events to fully cover the entire forum. It was not possible for me to get as intimately involved as I wished. This situation arose from my commitment to conduct the Greengrass seminars. As I mentioned earlier, the venue for the seminars was several miles away from the main action at Flamengo Park. Compounding the difficult access, the plans for free public bus transit to the out-of-park meetings fell through, and each person had to find their own way by transit in an area known for its street crime. A subway worker's strike further eroded the potential attendees to the Greengrass seminars.

Those that did attend were the dedicated, and the most knowledgeable about global environmental governance. Among them, several Latin American nations, concerned, and favorably disposed to act in support of global environmental protection. The delegates were mostly lawyer types from academia. Rather quickly, the debate ran past my competence and my understanding of legalese. It was clear to me, after assessing what had transpired in the nine seminars, that there was an enormous amount of work that still needed to be done before enforceable agreements to protect the global environment could occur. I came away from the seminars with the feeling that perhaps by the time enforceable agreements are reached, this poor beleaguered planet will be spinning through space, gray and desolate: those left, fighting one another for the basics of life.

A terrible depression seemed about to overwhelm me. Instead of finding solutions, I found that the global situation was really much worse than I had thought. Nation-states were, with very few exceptions, not willing to do what was deemed necessary to halt and reverse the destruction of Earth's ecosystems.

As to public awareness, there were those who knew the problems and wanted to address them in a creative, solution oriented, manner; those who didn't know, or didn't care, about the state of the environment; and those who knew and refused to make, or implement, the changes necessary. The latter group, primarily bureaucracies and elected politicians, represented the vast middle who when polled, agreed that something needed to be done to protect the environment, but when asked about specific measures and the possible economic consequences for them, were not supportive. Hence, the need for a strong collective voice insisting upon ecosystem preservation, must be kept front and center, regardless. The war to preserve the Earth's ecosystems must continue, everywhere—globally, locally, and within one's self.

Greenpeace played a popular visible role at the Global Forum. The Greenpeace flagship *Rainbow Warrior* was docked alongside the nearby Hotel Gloria pier, immediately adjacent to Flamengo Park. The vessel was fitted with an assembly hall in the hold. There, a visual display of the Greenpeace activities that had taken place over the years was displayed.

The captain of the *Rainbow Warrior* designated 'open ship' from mid-morning to supper time. Literally hundreds of people stood in line for hours, in the steaming heat, to get a chance to visit the boat. Aware of the bombing of the original *Rainbow Warrior* in Auckland, the Government of Brazil dispatched an armed guard to regulate access.

I was not about to stand in line to board the vessel. With the authority of long standing Greenpeace involvement, I approached the gangplank and in my bad Portuguese requested permission to board. I was refused. I informed one of the troopers that I was the 'Papa of Greenpeace.' They either didn't understand me, or more probably didn't care. Somewhat disappointed, but reassured that this *Rainbow Warrior* would be adequately protected, I turned back, and unwilling to wait in line, left the pier. Still, it was heartwarming to have experienced the great public interest in Greenpeace in this, more or less, isolated part of the world.

This interest of the ordinary people of Rio in Greenpeace came as a bit of a surprise. I had thought that awareness of the need to preserve the environment would be fairly low on the totem pole of concerns of the people of Brazil. I did not anticipate the strength and dedication of Greenpeace Brazil and the Brazilian Green Party. Previously, I was certain that concern for the environment was a northern nation middle-class movement. I was not prepared for the grassroots activism of the people of Brazil. Together, with my experience gained during the Greengrass seminars, I was amazed to find that all of Latin America was in ferment about the rapid deterioration of their natural environment.

Demonstration of this concern became evident shortly after U.S. president Bush refused to attend the formal UNCED proceedings with the statement that: "I will not participate in any meeting which presumes to reduce the standard of living of the American people." The reaction to that statement was swift. Thousands of Rio's citizens, trade unions, and other non-Government organizations massed in the streets outside Government buildings in downtown Rio and burned effigies of George Bush. The morning after, a parade of more than 10,000 persons marched the length of Avenue Atlantico to the headquarters of the UNCED officialdom. There, they set up a platform and for hours, speaker after speaker, denounced the position taken by the Government of the United States.

I had my day down to a routine: up each morning at 6:00a.m.; eat breakfast, and by taxi, go to Flamengo Park. Distribute notices for Greengrass seminars on global environmental governance; walk to the subway to downtown Rio; then to Banco do Brazil, sidestepping pickpockets and various panhandlers along the way; set up the visual aids in the conference room; and await the participants for 9:00a.m. At noon, the seminar would be over, and I would pack my attache case and be off to the Central Press Office.

I was somewhat disappointed at first by the absence of the advertised experts in the field of global governance. Hilary French, of the prestigious Worldwatch Institute, was the author of an excellent paper on global environmental governance. Bill Pace was with a legal firm in

Washington, DC, and was the expert on intergovernmental affairs for UNCED. And Bill Hudson, a World Federalist, had considerable experience in global governance. They had promised to appear and contribute to the Greengrass seminars. In attempting to track down these three, I learned that Hudson was delayed by several days in reaching Rio, and Pace was heavily involved in assisting the official UNCED delegates to frame the text of a proposed Commission for Sustainable Development. I could not locate the whereabouts of French, except that several people thought that she did not attend the UNCED deliberations.

In some ways, I was rather relieved that they did not participate. There were so few attendees. Their absence also served to give me more time to present the arguments for a global green constitution.

The Central Press building was just a few blocks outside of Flamengo Park. I had gained official access due to my Knowledge Network credentials. The facilities there were extensive and sophisticated. I was able to type, print, and distribute news releases concerning the activities of the Greengrass Institute seminars. This printed material was made available to the more than 3,000 members of the global press. News of what Greengrass was doing made the Rio papers and, so I am told, fairly well reported elsewhere in the world. Media coverage couldn't be better.

Reflections

After the full two-week exposure to the ideas of thousands and the discussions with hundreds of people at the Forum, I experienced what amounted to a 'sea change' in my way of thinking. Prior to the Rio experience I had not given much thought to the obvious fact that unless there was substantial improvement of the economic welfare of the poor in all nations, there would never be global ecosystem protection. The rural poor, especially, faced with increasingly desperate circumstances, would press wildlife habitats to extinction in order to obtain some measure of material stability.

To accomplish this task will require a shift in national policies to a point where the organizing principle of governance shifts from a policy of creating opportunity to gratify greed, to that of satisfying need.

Actualization of a transition in national policy from resource exploitation to sustainability will require about 50 years to take root and flower. I believe that a good portion of society, rich and poor, will embrace the shift in policy. The main question now involves the transition and what will occur during the intervening 50 years. In that time interval Planet Earth will be called upon to yield ever increasing rates of wildlife habitat loss and resource depletion. This onslaught *must* be minimized wherever possible. This task of preventing habitat loss ought to be the central objective of conservation organizations and progressive political parties.

NGOs have to become involved with the United Nations process of promoting democratization of all nations, and in the restructuring of UN decision making processes along the lines of the Euro-parliament. Greenpeace and others need to help set up conservation organizations all over the world, and train their activists in the vagaries of non-violent direct action.

Education of the young is crucial. Unfortunately, the youth of today are exposed to many other influences, mostly based on consumption of goods and services, and in being trained to compete in the job market. And too, the decisions to commit to ecosystem protection must be made prior to the time when the youth of today mature and are prepared to take their place in the decision-making power structure. The destruction of habitat and wanton exploitation of resources must be stopped *now*.

Strategists at Greenpeace have always made the effort to gain maximum media attention, and to advertise the message in unambiguous terms about what this, or that, campaign wants to convey. Thus, in a larger sense, Greenpeace is an educational institution aimed at the general public. The inclusion of non-violent direct action campaigns mark the degree and extent of Greenpeace personnel's commitment to their cause.

That this approach is highly effective can be demonstrated in recalling a TV call-in program on the Jack Webster show, a CTV (Canadian) late afternoon program. Mr. Webster was known for his ability to promote controversy in an effort to stimulate call-ins. It was in the mid-80s. Greenpeace was conducting an on-going campaign of confronting naval vessels that were suspected of carrying nuclear weapons into the port of Vancouver. Activists were navigating fast Zodiac rubber boats in front of, and alongside of, U.S. aircraft carriers, attempting to board them and often being repulsed by sailors wielding high pressure water hoses.

After one of these actions Jack Webster invited me to appear on his public affairs call-in TV network program. Webster's workstation at the TV studio was hooked up to a large bank of call waiting devices with blinking red lights indicating a backlog of citizen's interest. At the beginning of the program, Jack and I chatted about Greenpeace in general and about confronting the U.S. Navy in particular. We noted that no calls were coming in.

Eventually, Webster asked me what was so special about Greenpeace. Why was the organization so popular with the public? In reply, I explained that nearly every Greenpeace activist was willing to risk his/her life when they took part in a direct action. Not more than ten seconds later the whole display of call-waiting lights turned red.

Webster was practically speechless at the enormous response. And incidentally, not one caller had anything derogatory to say about Greenpeace. Some callers were not particularly turned on by Greenpeace's attempted blockading of warships entering Vancouver harbour, but all were touched by the sincerity of the protester's dedication in being willing to risk their personal safety on behalf of *la causa*.

I have spent the last forty years or so jousting with the human forces that are destroying nature. The environmental activist community has won many battles, but we are still losing the war. It would be seriously delusional to claim a fundamental change in the status quo.

In the span of nearly half a century world population has doubled, resource extraction has quadrupled, and virtually all wild animal habitats have been seriously compromised. Despite the adoption of the Comprehensive Test Ban Treaty in September 1996, and some progress in nuclear disarmament *via* the Strategic Arms Limitation Treaty, there are enough remaining nuclear armaments and delivery systems to destroy the world.

Part of the reason for such minimal success is that no group inside, or outside, of the environmental community, with the exception of the World Federalists, has grasped the fundamental reality that all nation-states must relinquish sufficient sovereignty to a system of global environmental governance to ensure that life on Planet Earth will not be diminished or put at risk by human actions. I have underscored the sense of urgency, and initiated a debate concerning the critical need for global environmental governance, by including in this book my essay "Towards a Global Green Constitution." This document was widely circulated in 1991 to the relevant experts in the United Nations system. It was made available to the many thousands of participants at the UNCED Rio 1992 conference.

A metaphor for the situation in which we presently find ourselves can be found in the fate of the *Titanic*. The most powerful, the largest oceangoing craft ever built went headlong in pursuit of its objective to set a speed record across the Atlantic Ocean. Defying the forecasted presence of icebergs in its path the great ship struck a massive ice sheet. In less than two hours the triumph of western technology was on the bottom of the ocean. It didn't carry sufficient lifeboats because no one felt that they were required in view of the unsinkable design.

Let us not abandon this Earth to a similar fate.

EPILOGUE:
GREENPEACE NOW AND THEN

Greenpeace experienced a drop in absolute numbers of supporters from a high of 3.5 million in 1989, to 2.5 million by 1998. The reduction in support was, in part, due to the Establishment undertaking a campaign of what the environmental community called 'greenwash.' Simply put, industry equated protection of the environment with a loss of jobs: an argument that scared off support for environmental organizations.

Greenpeace responded with two major actions: one, was to convince existing supporters to give more money; the second, was to globalize campaigns in an attempt to level the playing field with the multinationals. Both strategies were successful.

Although financial support decreased by almost one-third, it was more than made up for by a huge increase in the amount that donors were contributing. Greenpeace reorganized internally and in the process found itself financially positioned to conduct high profile global campaigns.

One example was the war in the woods that squarely pitted the huge forest industry against the environmental community in the Clayoquot Sound region on the west coast of Canada. Greenpeace campaigners undertook a world-wide boycott of coastal British Columbia lumber to pressure industry to give up the ecologically devastating practice of clear-cutting and switch to selection logging. In 1988, after a five-year campaign, one of the worlds largest forest companies agreed to halt clear-cutting. This capitulation by industry demonstrated the effectiveness of the Greenpeace led global boycott.

The next step was to discourage the forest industry from moving its logging activities to other countries where less pressure to do ecologically based logging was expected. (Greenpeace and others are taking steps to prevent this by helping to establish the Forest Stewardship Council [FSC] which is fostering ecologically appropriate uses of forested land everywhere. An action functing much like a boycott, large consumers of forest products, such as Home Depot, have agreed to refuse to purchase lumber that is not certified by the Forest Stewardship Council. As of this writing, scores of forest industry corporations, large and small, are requesting FSC certification applications.)

The 1999 Battle of Seattle, by 50,000 people objecting to World Trade Organization (WTO) practices, was a hallmark of common cause by the environmental movement, the social justice movement, and the trade union movement: the trade union movement now understands that a depleted environment results in loss of jobs; the social justice movement understands that the bottom line of trans-national corporations obliges the poor to live adjacent to the toxic effluvia spewed out when they cross borders to obtain cheap sources of labour and are allowed to function with a blind eye to whatever pollution controls exist; and the environmental community now realizes that the progressive movements are interdependent.

The future of Greenpeace can be reasonably predicted from an analysis of its major accomplishments during the first half of its existence (1971-1984), and during the second half (1985-1998). According to the "Record of Achievement," listed in the 1998 Greenpeace International annual report, eight 'wins' were indicated for the first half, and 64 during the second half. The magnitude of this success rate can be further illustrated by the fact that in 1998 there were 18 'wins' or as many in a single year as there were in total from its first campaign in 1971 through 1992, a span of 21 years.

This tremendous growth stems from an increasing competence in campaigning and administration. It is also a measure of a deteriorating planet. As conditions worsen Greenpeace-like movements will grow.

Greenpeace and the Green Party

The manifesto of the Ecology Party, which is the former name of the United Kingdom Green Party, states in its introduction that Greenpeace actions inspired the formation of their Party. Greenpeace also inspired hundreds of people to take an active part in campaigning for ecological protection and in attracting thousands of others in supporting roles.

It seems logical to assume that Greenpeace and the various Green Parties would work together—even to affiliate in some form. Geopolitical realities prevent any formal association. Greenpeace operates globally and seamlessly. Green Parties function in nation-states attempting to convince a mostly reluctant electorate to cast votes for green candidates.

Globally, Green Party entities appear sporadically and with varying degrees of electoral success. It is difficult to envision an effective global association of Green Parties, since it faces the same potential for divisiveness as is experienced at the United Nations. Similarly, Greenpeace would not consider adopting the idea of a Global Green Constitution. If they did adopt it, they would be obliged to entertain campaigning on social and economic issues, such as a guaranteed annual income for all. They are simply not prepared to expand their commitments, for the Greenpeace plate is more than full.

Towards Global Green Governance

For the past ten years I have served on the governing council of the World Federalists of Canada. Although I have many reservations about world government, I maintain that ecological sustainability can only occur if it is addressed globally and adequately enforced. Clearly Greenpeace cannot act as the law enforcement agency of the eco-world—nor can any other non-government organization. Global problems have to be addressed globally. National, ethnic, and cultural barriers exist to prevent the imposition of global governance.

As the natural environment inexorably deteriorates, and its adverse effects become evident to the most recalcitrant foot-draggers, perhaps that will prompt nation-state Governments to relinquish some of their sovereignty and accept global green governance.

Some Predictions

As Greenpeace and other environmental organizations gain in size and respect, their heightened campaign activity will increase attention to the plight of the planet, improving the electoral prospects for Green Parties everywhere.

The Greens will present a workable economic platform that is inclusive, and based upon quality rather than quantity oriented lifestyles.

Green politicians will take office in those democracies which have electoral systems based on proportional representation and will help to form majority coalition governments, as have the Die Grunen in Germany.

The next United Nations Conference on Environment and Development will probably take place during 2012. I expect that the notion of a Global Green Constitution will be seriously explored, and possibly enacted, by a majority of the nations represented. The Greengrass Institute will actively participate in this endeavor.

The United Nations General Assembly will consist of members elected by a parliamentary majority, rather than the present method by which heads of state appoint the delegates. This will lead to more informed decisions and render ratification of progressive measures more likely to occur.

As a consequence of general disenchantment about various global entities such as NAFTA, the WTO, INF, and the World Bank, their work will become more transparent and inclusive of the general public. The most pressing issue—the loss of jobs due to exporting them to less developed nations—will be ameliorated by higher wages and better working conditions in the developing nations and adequate redundancy pay for the displaced worker community.

There is plenty of evidence which suggests an impending ecological collapse. It will surely overwhelm us sooner or later if we ignore the symptoms and keep on doing 'business as usual.'

However, if we accept the challenge, address needs, rather than greeds, live lifestyles of quality rather than quantity, and get on with the job, Planet Earth may recover, may forgive. Over time, its resilience and our care may enable a sustainable future for all.

APPENDIX: THE CANNIKIN TEST

A Critical Look at Some of the Justifications and Risks Associated with the 5-Megaton Nuclear Test on Amchitka Island, Alaska, prepared for the Don't Make a Wave Committee, by Robert J. Keziere, August, 1971

In the fall of 1971, probably October, the United States Atomic Energy Commission plans to detonate a 5-megaton hydrogen bomb some 6,000 feet beneath the island of Amchitka in Alaska. Amchitka, located 1,500 miles from Kodiak near the western end of the Aleutian chain, is a part of the Aleutian Islands National Wildlife Refuge. The island is situated almost immediately above the great Aleutian Fault in an area that yearly experiences several earthquakes of Richter magnitude 6.0 or greater.

Upon President Richard Nixon's approval, the proposed test, code name Cannikin, will become the third nuclear device to be detonated under Amchitka. The test that results will involve the most powerful underground nuclear explosion that has been detonated by the United States Government.

The growing public awareness of the problems precipitated by nuclear weapons testing has in recent years led to considerable general opposition, notably with respect to the Amchitka tests. At the time of AEC's second detonation, Milrow, in October 1969, the nationwide protest of 18,000 Canadians effectively closed the 4,000 mile

Canada-USA border for the first time since the war of 1812. Following this action, the Don't Make a Wave Committee was established in Vancouver in an effort to facilitate continued opposition to the testing of nuclear weapons. The organizations endorsing the Committee are:

The Association of Western Canadian Universities

The B.C. Conference of the United Church of Canada

The Canadian Voice of Women

The Sierra Club of B.C.

The Sierra Club Pacific Northwest Chapter

The Society for Pollution and Environmental Control (B.C.)

Pollution Probe of Ontario

Student Societies of all Western Canadian Universities

The B.C. Federation of Labour

Vancouver and District Labour Council

The B.C. Building and Trades Council etc.

B.C. Environmental Council

Through the above organizations, and other groups (and individuals) too numerous to mention, over 100,000 Canadians support the Don't Make a Wave Committee in its attempt to translate growing public opposition to continued nuclear testing into meaningful government action.

The committee, incorporated under the Societies Act of British Columbia, has as its registered objects, the fostering of public awareness of the possible environmental effects of the detonation of nuclear explosives, and the support of conduct of research in the area of environmental preservation. The committee is on public record as being unconditionally opposed to testing of nuclear weapons by anyone, anywhere, anytime. The pending Amchitka test fits squarely into this category!

This paper, prepared for the Don't Make a Wave Committee, is a review of the available and pertinent literature concerning the principal issues involved in the ongoing nuclear testing at the AEC's Amchitka Island test site.

The Issues

In essence, the question to test or not involves two opposing considerations:

(1) Clearly, American defense policy has for some time been heavily committed to the development and deployment of nuclear weapons as the principal means of affecting and maintaining national security. It comes as no surprise that such policy, given a corresponding Soviet defense policy, necessitates the continuous development and stock-piling of nuclear weapons.

(2) The U.S. nuclear defense policy has intrinsically associated with it a number of risks which obviously must be borne by all mankind. Nuclear war not withstanding, the unquestionable titan is the introduction, assimilation and subsequent effect of radioactive materials on the biosphere, present and future.

We are asked to accept the risks in return for the benefit of national security. What specifically are the risks and the benefits of the Amchitka nuclear test program?

The Benefits, Are They Real?

In deference to the U.S. National Environmental Policy Act of 1969, the AEC held public hearings on May 26th and 28th, 1971, in Juneau and Anchorage, Alaska, respectively. In a statement at the hearings, General Giller, representing the AEC, indicated the reason for AEC's underground nuclear tests:

> In order to provide for the nation's security and to assist in providing for the security of the rest of the free world, it is the policy of the United States to maintain a strong nuclear force to discourage attack by any potential aggressor.

Only through technological advancement can we provide an effective nuclear force to counter potential actions by others. Accordingly, testing is essential for providing these technological advances—from the testing of new concepts to the testing of finished weapons.

The AEC's Redraft Cannikin Environmental Statement of April 30, 1971, under the heading of "Why Cannikin?," stated simply: "Cannikin is an underground nuclear test which is a vital part of the weapons development program of the United States."

As indicated in a recent article in *Science* (June 18, 1971), critics of AEC programs have traditionally encountered difficulty in effectively attacking the AEC's national security justification, principally due to the normally classified nature of the intended use of the nuclear device being tested. However, it has been public knowledge for some time (recently officially confirmed by the AEC), that the 5-megaton Cannikin device is to be employed as the warhead on the ABM Spartan missiles. These missiles are long-range interceptors fitted with very large warheads of several megatons. They were designed (in 1964) to destroy a light attack (Chinese) of incoming ballistic missiles while the latter were still outside the atmosphere. In principal, with no more than fifteen Spartan interceptor batteries it was considered possible to defend the entire coterminous of the United States against nuclear attack by the Chinese.

However, in a statement before the Anchorage Cannikin hearings, Dr. Jeremy J. Stone, Director of the prestigious Federation of American Scientists severely criticized the necessity of the Cannikin test on the grounds that the necessity of the Spartan ABM system as originally proposed has been seriously undermined since the AEC's start on the Cannikin project. Therefore, it is worthwhile to consider briefly the history of the Spartan system.

In 1967 the Johnson administration announced plans to build the ABM Spartan system and at, or around, this time the AEC began work on Cannikin. By 1969 the Nixon administration had reviewed the ongoing

ABM program, and emphasized that ABM's (Spartan included) primary purpose was the defense of the Minuteman ICBMs; the defense of the U.S. cities from Chinese attack was regarded as a supplemental purpose and future option.

In 1970, the Senate Armed Services Committee expressed its disapproval of the anti-Chinese Spartan system by cutting funds for the Spartan land-sites. The Spartan was further undermined upon the recent Department of Defense announcement of its intention to develop an "Improved Spartan." The Improved Spartan, according to the D.O.D. as quoted in Dr. Stone's paper,

> ...will carry a smaller warhead (than the basic Spartan) but to much higher velocities.

The Improved Spartan does not require Cannikin.

Finally, on May 20th of 1971, President Nixon announced a U.S. and Soviet agreement to "concentrate efforts this year" on a treaty limiting ABM systems. Such limitation would simply restrict the numbers of ABM sites to capital cities or other specific strategic sites, such as Minuteman ICBM fields. According to Dr. Stone:

> ...none of the alternatives for limited ABM's being discussed at SALT (Strategic Arms Limitation Talks) require the basic Spartan.

He continues:

> In addition, the President's announcement on May 19th of a hopefully imminent agreement on SALT, that would limit ABM's, has important implications for this nuclear test. The SALT agreement would limit numbers of interceptors and force the Defense planners to choose between Sprints, Basic Spartans and Improved Spartans. Under these circumstances they might well choose to buy no Basic Spartans at all. Many Defense planners believe that, in essence, there is nothing important which Basic Spartan can do that Improved Spartan cannot do better. In short, the President's announcement represents an important new reason

for deferring Cannikin until we discover whether SALT agreement can be reached this year, (1971) as seems to be expected by the administration.

The Federation of American Scientists' critique goes further, but suffice it to say here they conclude that Cannikin is basically a "bureaucratic oversight" that should have been canceled by the Nixon administration in 1969 when the rationale concerning the specific uses of the ABM Basic Spartan system were changed.

Before leaving the question of national security, specifically with respect to Cannikin, mention should be made of the more general consideration expressed by Herbert York, who was the D.O.D. Director of Defense Research and Engineering from 1958-1961. York, among others, contends that far from increasing national security, the ABM's and other weapons are in fact decreasing the security.

> Ever since World War II, the military power of the U.S. has been steadily increasing; over the same period the national security has been rapidly and inexorably diminishing... It is my view that the problem...has no tactical solution. If we continue to look for solutions in the area of military science and technology only, the result will be a steady and inexorable worsening of the situation. (*Race to Oblivion*, 1970, p.21-22; as quoted in Explanation Concerning Environmental Statement, by Egan O'Connor)

Harold Brown, York's successor in the D.O.D. position, and later Secretary of the Air Force, supported this position:

> We must seek national security through other than strictly military means...and urgently. (*Race to Oblivion*, p.23)

Also,

> I am sure that unless we nerve ourselves to make the attempt (to rollback arms and agree on disarmament), and make it soon, we are quite simply doomed. (York in *Life Magazine*, December 11, 1970)

In a critique of the AEC's Cannikin Environmental Impact Statement Egan O'Connor, atomic energy consultant to Alaskan Senator Mike Gravel, also expressed concern regarding this issue.

We have from men whose knowledge and patriotism is unquestionable, and whose judgment was respected so highly that they were appointed to these positions of high responsibility (referring to York, Brown, and others), that the Cannikin weapon is obsolete and the development of such weapons systems are positively harmful to our national security.

It is obvious that, as long as we go along with the premise that our security can be increased and won by weapons, we will postpone consideration of humane ways to deal with human conflict.

It is equally obvious that the only way to be sure that nuclear weapons are never used—which is what we profess to want—is not to have them around.

It is equally obvious that you don't build nuclear weapons systems at all unless there are conditions under which you are willing to use them. Under what circumstances do the American people want to incinerate the Russian people?

Before we take any risks at all for Cannikin, we are entitled to know and to debate the question of whether as a people, we want to use the weapon under any circumstances.

Assuming that retaliation is the appropriate, humane, mature response to an attack we failed to prevent on ourselves, assuming that there is some issue between Russia and the United States that the American people are willing to massacre millions over...why Cannikin?

The point at hand is that the overall concept of developing and deploying nuclear weapons systems as a principal means of maintaining national security has undergone substantial re-evaluation by a number of the U.S.

administrators, scientists, and most notably by high ranking officials within the U.S. Department of Defense itself. The AEC's critical assertion that Cannikin is "vital to our national security" must be regarded in recognizance of these considerations. At present, it would appear that the benefit of the Cannikin weapon as regards national security is fundamentally questionable.

Other Justifications

The preceding section outlined in some detail the controversial national security question with the testing of nuclear weapons generally and Cannikin specifically. Clearly, numerous considerations other than national security, *per se*, must bear on the necessity of the Cannikin event. Time and source limitations, within respect to this paper, are of necessity limiting, however, as an attempt at completeness, several of the more obvious influences are briefly considered below.

It has recently been acknowledged by the AEC that the Nevada Test Site has proven to be unsafe as regards the underground detonation of greater than 1-megaton nuclear weapons. Dr. William E. Ogle of the Los Alamos Scientific Laboratory, testifying on behalf of the AEC at the May 1971 Alaska Environmental Hearings clearly indicated the AEC's desire to establish an alternative underground test site which would accommodate nuclear weapons tests more powerful than 1-megaton.

Previous to the Nuclear Test Ban Treaty of 1963, the United States tested many devices of yields appreciably greater than Milrow (one megaton); however, we had not had experience with large yield shots underground. During the 1960s a proving ground was developed in Nevada that was good for yields slightly greater than a megaton but clearly could not go appreciably larger. (To date, 1971, the AEC have carried out 6, 1-megaton tests at NTS.)

The major problem with high yield detonations in Nevada is that the modern high rise buildings of Las Vegas resonate due to the ground motion produced by very large shots. Predictions were that for somewhat larger detonations that motion could cause structural damage. When it became clear in 1966 or 1967 that there were overwhelming reasons for the United States to conduct tests in an energy region larger than were safe at the Nevada Test Site, the test organization conducted an extensive survey of all those regions available to the United States to fire larger underground shots.

Dr. Ogle indicated that twenty-four potential locations were seriously considered. These candidates, principally sites on the continental United States, were narrowed to three: (1) a Nevada site somewhat north of the present NTS; (2) a site in the Brooks Mountain Range, Alaska; (3) and Amchitka Island. It was from a consideration of the latter three that the Amchitka Island Site was selected.

If one accepts the proposition that sometime in the future the United States will feel required to test greater than 1-megaton nuclear devices, it seems there can be little if any reasonable doubt that such testing will be carried out at Amchitka. To date, the AEC have issued no meaningful comments concerning the subject of future tests on Amchitka.

An extensive search for an underground test site suitable for large yield nuclear devices has turned up Amchitka. Reasonably, to the extent the Cannikin test can contribute, politically and economically, to the establishment of an on-going test site program, the Cannikin event would be of value to the AEC.

It would be difficult indeed for the layman to accurately gauge the political consequences of the 5-megaton Cannikin tests, say specifically with respect to the SALT talks or the domestic scene prior to the 1972 Presidential elections, or to Nixon's forthcoming visit to China. From the Nixon administration's viewpoint, the continuation of the Alaska test might well be regarded as a necessity relative to these political arenas. Indeed, in the final analysis the political consequences seem paramount.

Robert J. Basell in *Science* June 18, 1971, reports:

The Undersecretaries Committee of the National Security Council, which consists of Presidential Assistant Henry Kissinger and representatives of the State Department, the Joint Chiefs of Staff, and the Central Intelligence Agency is conducting a detailed study to counsel the President in his decision on whether or not to proceed with the test. Advising the committee for this study are representatives of the Arms Control and Disarmament Agency, the Office of Management and Budget, the Council on Environmental Quality, the AEC, and the Department of the Interior. According to reliable Administration sources, the study will make no recommendation because there is no consensus either for or against conducting the test.

But the purpose of the report is not to weigh the need for the weapon against the possible environmental consequences. Rather, it will concentrate on the possible political consequences for Nixon if he goes ahead with the test or if he cancels it.

At this writing (August 3, 1971), the U.S. Congress and Senate have effectively relegated the final yes-no-postpone decision to President Nixon. The President has as yet to make his decision public.

The Risks, Are They Real?

It would probably be instructive to describe the phenomenology associated with the deep underground detonation of a large yield nuclear weapon. Such a discussion, it is hoped, would perhaps facilitate a better understanding of the risks involved in the Cannikin test.

According to a paper by Dr. James E. Carothers, Lawrence Radiation Laboratory, presented to the May 1971 Alaska hearings, the Cannikin device will be detonated at the bottom of an emplacement hole, 90-inches in diameter and 5,875-feet deep. In addition, two other holes have been drilled in conjunction with the test: instrument and de-watering holes. Both of the latter are at least as deep as the emplacement shaft. At the time of detonation, all three holes will have been "appropriately" sealed; the emplacement shaft with alternating sections of 1,000 feet of pea gravel and 50-foot long coal-tar-epoxy plugs; the instrument and de-watering holes with cement and high pressure oil field plugs, respectively.

The following is a somewhat lengthy, but enlightening, quote from Dr. Carother's Alaska hearings paper entitled, "Cannikin Predictions for Containment and Phenomenology":

> Now let us look at what happens when a 5-megaton nuclear device is detonated more than a mile underground in a thick layer of basalt. When the nuclear device is detonated, the energy equivalent to the detonation of 5 million tons of TNT is released in millionths of a second.

> The material in the nuclear device is vaporized instantly and raised to a temperature of several million degrees. A strong shock wave moves out from this source and vaporizes the surrounding rock in a few thousandths of a second. At this point, a cavity has been formed having a diameter of about 200 feet and containing rock vapor at a pressure of 15-million pounds per square inch. The cavity continues to expand initially by melting the rock on the cavity walls and then by simply pushing the cavity walls outward until the pressure in the cavity drops to a value equal to 6,000 pounds per square inch which is roughly the pressure exerted by the weight of the rock above the cavity. The cavity will grow in this way to a diameter of 800-feet. While the cavity is growing, the main shock from the detonation is moving toward the surface. It arrives at about the time the cavity stops growing and causes the surface to rise momentarily about 20-feet into the air. These then are the early time effects of a nuclear detonation. It is all over in a few seconds.

> The situation after these early time effects have taken place is that underground we have a cavity full of high temperature rock vapor

at a pressure of 6,000 pounds per square inch while on the surface we may have a permanent uplift of as much as a few feet over a large area surrounding ground zero. I will not discuss movement on existing faults due to the detonation as other speakers will cover that in detail.

Our calculations indicated that the underground cavity will stand as is for a few hours. The molten rock will of course flow down the walls and rain off the roof forming a puddle of molten rock in the bottom of the 800-foot diameter explosion cavity. All of this time the cavity gases are cooling by simple heat transfer to the walls of the cavity. After a few hours, the temperature drops to the point that the rock gases condense into molten rock which coats the cavity walls and then flows into the puddle. The transfer of heat into the surrounding rock through the cavity walls results in a large difference in temperature in the rock layers immediately surrounding the cavity which causes the cracking and flaking of the rock on the cavity surface. This enhances the cooling rate as these pieces of rock fall into the puddle cooling it to the point it begins to fuse and also exposing cooler rock on the cavity walls which reduces the temperature of the remaining gases. Continued cooling leads to the condensing of such condensable gases as water vapor. Of course, at this time, the temperature and pressure is well below that imposed by the overburden. The cavity roof can no longer support itself and it collapses onto the fused glass on the cavity floor. The collapse continues upward in a few seconds through the material cracked by the explosion and forms a chimney of rubble. The rubble quenches the remaining condensable gases in the cavity. If the chimney does not encounter a rock layer strong enough to support the remaining overburden as it spans the top of the chimney, collapse will continue to the surface. We do not believe that in the case in point, or in Cannikin, that the collapse would stop before it reaches the surface. As the collapse proceed to the surface, it does so in its own good time. We cannot predict with any certainty when it will reach the surface. It probably will occur within a few days but it could take weeks or even months. As it collapses toward the surface, we expect the chimney to open outwards. Our prediction of the contour of the surface after collapse reaches it is that we will have a depression about a mile in diameter going from a depth of zero at the edge to about 50-feet in the center.

There are essentially four vital problems which may arise subsequent to an event such as the one described above:

(1) Ultimately, containment of the nuclear explosion may prove unsuccessful. An atmospheric, or ocean venting leak would of course introduce radioactive materials into the biosphere, resulting in the spectrum of well-documented toxic effects.

(2) The blast induced shock waves could seriously threaten the surrounding ecological environment, an approximately 60-year old National Wildlife Refuge.

(3) It is considered by seismic authorities that it is finitely probable that the principal shock wave could trigger a natural earthquake of Richter magnitude greater than the induced seismic shock.

(4) The shock effects of the detonation pose the threat of generating a destructive tsunami sea wave. Tsunamis resulting from natural earthquakes in the Aleutians have caused extensive damage as far away as California and Hawaii. (*Science*, June 18, 1971)

The Problem of Containment of Radioactivity

Despite the AEC's sophisticated precautions and continued assurances as to the "negligible," "highly improbable" and "vanishingly small" possibility of venting or leaking of a nuclear weapons test, the record of such occurrences is not at all compelling. Of the 230 underground tests performed at the Nevada Test Site, 67 have leaked measurable amounts of radioactivity. (*Science*, June18, 1971) This is 29 percent. O'Connor in the Cannikin Critique previously quoted, indicates that 16 were detected beyond the test site boundaries; 11 more leaked enough to be detected beyond ground zero, but not beyond the Test Site. In addition, about 40 tests leaked radioactivity detected only in the 'immediate vicinity' of the firing point. (These figures from AEC Chairman Seaborg to Senator Gravel, March 11, 1971.) O'Connor, in the Cannikin Critique, has summarized concern regarding containment of the high yielding test:

On page 12, 'adequate distance from faults' is listed as a requirement for assured containment of radioactivity.' On page 13, 'Cannikin site is 1,300 feet south of the Teal Creek Fault and 2,800 feet north of a suspected fault.' Also, according to the AEC Nevada release, May 1,4 (#NV-71-29) about the leaking test Baneberry, in December 1970, the leak did not occur through a fault. The test at 910 feet deep just split the Earth with its own pressure, which pressure exceeded expectations because 'the earth around the explosive device was more saturated with water than had been expected': water causes greatly increased pressure, which also lasts longer after the detonation. Cannikin is in water-saturated rock.

If little Baneberry (less than 20 kilotons) had enough power to 'force gas through the ground to the surface' 910 feet above, and open up a 'fissure 315 feet long,' what gives the AEC confidence that Cannikin in water-saturated rock can't push gas 2,800 feet to the suspected fault? If they failed to detect the pocket of underground water in Nevada, 'in an area of the test site where two other tests had been conducted previously with no problems,' what surprises lay undetected on Amchitka? Water pockets? Unsuspected faults? Sonic mapping of faults is effective/reliable to what depth?

Banebury, it might be noted, vented a cloud of debris thousands of feet into the air, spreading radioactive material over several Canadian

Provinces and 13 U.S. states. While the Canadian Government does not officially regard the event as a violation of the Test Ban Treaty, radiation was recorded in Fort William, Ottawa, Toronto and Montreal. (*Environment*, April 1970)

In a communication from AEC Chairman Seaborg to Senator Gravel (March 11, 1971) the AEC indicated that 3 million curies were released into the air, which "possibly contained 100 percent of the Krypton-88 and 100 percent of the Tritium" inventory.

Interestingly, the first test on Amchitka, carried out quite secretively by the Department of Defense, also leaked. The 80-kiloton Longshot was detonated on October 29, 1965. By October 1969, small concentrations of tritium (radioactive hydrogen) had migrated sufficiently to be observed in local surface ponds around ground zero of the Longshot test site. The AEC asserts that the concentrations involved are well below the recommended concentration guides (RCG), which directs the discussion to consideration of the principal harmful radio-nuclides probably involved, their associated toxicity, and the controversy regarding the "dilution" of radioactive substances.

While the AEC's Environmental Impact Statement did not discuss specifically the biologically important radio-nuclide inventory, previous evidence would indicate the following: strontium-90 (half life 28.1 years); iodine-131 (8.07 days); cesium-137 (30.2 years); carbon-14 (5730 years) and tritium (12.26 years).

An extremely critical consideration here is that of the order of 100 half-lives are required to effect essentially complete decay of a given radioactive element. Thus, implicit in the ultimate containment of radioisotopes generated in underground nuclear tests is the fact that the area surrounding the detonation zero point must remain seismically and otherwise unmolested for somewhere in the order of 100,000 years!

The hazards of these radioisotopes came to the public's attention largely through the efforts of Linus Pauling during the mid-1950s. At this time, Pauling with over 11,000 other scientists expressed their concern regarding the danger to the health and heredity of all living species on Earth. The 1963 Geneva Test Ban Treaty put an end to atmospheric testing by the United States, the USSR, and Great Britain. China and France are not signators. (A total of some 500 megatons were detonated in the atmosphere prior to 1963, [O'Connor, AEC Critique, 1971], and this figure does not include the current on-going series of 6 atmospheric tests being performed by the French Government.)

Dr. Leonard A. Walker, an internationally recognized radiation biologist and former consultant in radio-medicine to the Swedish Atomic Energy Commission (1962-1964, and currently a research professor at the University of B.C.), has expressed the concern of many informed scientific sources. In a statement read to the May 1971 Alaska Cannikin Hearings, Dr. Walker outlined some of the potential hazards:

We assume that elaborate safety precautions are planned to prevent a leak and to monitor the test site for leaks after the explosion. However, if anything unexpected happens and a leak occurs, it will be too late to do anything to prevent damage to the biosphere. All the best intentions, calculations, and predictions will not undo the permanent damage to the Earth's people and food supply. Even if quantitative data on monitoring were made public, it would not help to protect against the spread of radioactivity through the food chain and eventually into our bodies.

When dangerous isotopes such as strontium-90, carbon-14, tritium, etc., are released into the environment, even when they are scattered over hundreds of square miles of stratosphere, ocean or deep within the Earth, they are almost certain to eventually find their way into our food chain. We only rarely see the dramatic damage leading to death and devastation which occurs when large quantities of radioactive material are suddenly dumped upon the earth or sea. The long-term effects leading to stillbirths, hereditary defects, sterility, or death. The fact that these disastrous results may appear months or years later, or that they may be spread out over a number of generations does not make us less responsible. Calculations have been made, for example, of the number of thousands of children who will die of leukemia due to the release of a certain quantity of strontium-90. The exact number of thousands cannot, of course, be predicted with certainty but it is a certainty that these long term effects of radiation on man are real and deadly. I believe it is immoral to argue the relative statistics of these calculations when the qualitative facts are universally agreed upon by radiation biologists, and when the lives and health of many thousands of people are at stake.

Dr. John Gofman was formerly Associate Director of the AEC funded Lawrence Radiation Laboratory, and is currently Professor of Medical Physics at the University of California at Berkeley.

In the last year and a half, our own work, confirmed by other scientists, indicated that the production of cancer plus leukemia by radiation is some 20 to 30 times more severe than was thought by 'experts' less than a decade ago. The production of serious genetic disease, the result of radiation-induced mutations will, in all probability, be 50 times more severe than was thought by 'experts' less than a decade ago. Even though so-called 'peaceful atoms' programs are burgeoning rapidly, no real public indignation has occurred over the fact that we are allowed to get far more radiation than fallout produced ever, and the effect of each unit of radiation is 20-50 times as bad as most experts thought possible... Public indignation is exceedingly mild. We have a beginning of public awareness, but by no means commensurate with the hazard. (Public address, Vancouver, April 1971)

The concept of "recommended dilution guides," or safe levels of radiation has come under increasing attack from an international community of scientists. As is the case with a number of pesticides, mercury and other heavy metal compounds, it is now unquestionably a well documented scientific fact that many of the radioactive elements involved in this discussion tend to become concentrated by living organisms to magnify the isotopic concentration along a food chain, a low isotopic concentration at the point of introduction into the biosphere does not at all prevent the irreversible poisoning of the biosphere.

A final important consideration is the possible serious impact of a potential or actual contamination of the North Pacific salmon and shellfish, which are of paramount economic importance to Alaska—the USSR, Japan, Canada, other countries notwithstanding. According to Wallace A. Noerenberg, Commissioner, Alaska Department of Fish and Game, the dollar value (to the fishermen alone) of the Pacific salmon catch in 1970 was 60 million dollars. The corresponding total value for the king crab and other shellfish catch was 20.4 million.

> Amchitka Island lies in an ocean zone used extensively by important segments of the North Pacific anadromous salmon fisheries. Chum salmon from Honshu and Hokkaido Island of Japan and pink, chum and sockeye salmon from eastern Kamchatca Peninsula pass through the surrounding water of the island during both mature and immature stages of their life history. Aleutian and Bering Sea stocks of (U.S.) sockeye, pink, coho and king salmon also are known to be present in waters near the island as maturing and immature stages.

> The 'ownership' of salmon passing by Amchitka is thus international in scope and the consequences of any contamination of these animals would be worldwide in regard to marketing and human consumption problems.

> The Bristol Bay sockeye fishery of Alaska is the world's single most important fishery in value; these fish are particularly vulnerable at Amchitka since they migrate past the island on feeding and/or spawning migrations up to four times during their ocean life.

Should contamination of these salmon occur, the economic
disaster to one of Alaska's largest industries would be of a very
large magnitude. The value of pack from Bristol Bay salmon in
some years, e.g., 1970, approaches 50 percent of the total Alaska
pack value. (Noerenberg, Cannikin Hearings, Juneau, Alaska,)

It is interesting to contrast the above considerations with the fact that the
AEC's liability, under the Price-Anderson Act, is 500 million dollars.

Blast Impact Effect on the Ecology of Amchitka

The biology of Amchitka Island is relatively simple. The low-lying island
is about 42 miles long and averages 4 to 5 miles wide. Its highest point is
1,160 feet. It is covered with a tundra composed of grasses, sedges,
mosses, lichens and low shrubs. There are no noticeable trees, only a few
non-seeding Sitka Spruce brought in by the U.S. troops and a good deal of
prostrate willow. The shores are rocky and spectacular and life is oriented
towards the shores and the sea. For instance, 20 out of 27 species of birds
known to breed on the island are ducks and other water birds; 3 out of 5
species of fish found inland are ones which spend only part of their time
in fresh water. (M.L. Merritt, Sandia Laboratories, Alaska, 1971)

According to Noerenberg, "Amchitka Island is devoid of indigenous
land mammals (rats have been introduced)."

Fresh water fish species include Dolly Varden, stickleback, sculpini,
and immature populations of silver and red salmon. The avian
populations are more extensive and include 44 species of which 2 are on
the endangered list. The marine species in the environment, transient or
resident, include sea otter, sea lion, harbor seal, fur seal, whales, halibut,
king and tanner crab, herring and 5 species of salmon, previously
mentioned. Principal concern regarding the effect of the shock wave on
the ecology centers on the sea otter population. There are approaching
50,000 such animals in Alaska, with 4,000 otter at Amchitka. There are
other populations of sea otter in North America, however, the Alaska
otter represent a separate subspecies unique to these waters.

William Noerenberg summarized the Alaska Department of Fish and Game's concern:

> The AEC has established a 4-mile impact zone as the area that will be most affected by the event. They estimate that 10 percent of the sea otter found in the area will be susceptible to damaging pressures. The basis for these predictions seem to center on over-pressures of 150 pounds per square inch, damaging lungs. It is our opinion that ear drum damage leading to possible delayed mortality will occur at much lower pressures, and therefore more animals will be susceptible to detrimental impacts than indicated by the AEC.
>
> If eardrums are broken or damaged the animal's ability to dive is impaired—this could eventually lead to death by starvation.
>
> Another biologically significant consideration which the AEC has neglected to mention is the lack of any discussion or apparent consideration of the aspect of segregation of the sea otter sexes and the subsequent impact of the blast. Our data indicates that sea otters segregate by sex, and to a lesser degree by age. Females occupy the entire coast with a few non-breeding males. Sexually active males enter the area for breeding but they generally concentrate in "male areas" which are only a few hundred yards wide. There are probably no more than a half dozen such male areas on Amchitka. A single male area may contain most of the males from 15 miles of coast. There is one known male area, and a second possible area within the four mile zone of the blast. If a single segment of a population is severely damaged, the impact on the entire population is far more serious than if the damage is spread throughout all segments; it is more serious to kill 10 percent of the mature males in a population than it is to kill 10 percent of a mixed population.

There are approximately 350 seal and 75 sea-lions off Amchitka. Noerenberg indicated it was the Department of Fish and Game's opinion that the pressure effects would be as serious on these animals as on the otters, and that consequently, the AEC had underestimated the impact on these animals as well.

The Aleutian Earthquake Problem

It is well known from previous underground tests, both at the Nevada and Amchitka sites, that underground explosions regularly trigger earthquakes, sometimes in very large numbers and extending over a period of weeks or months subsequent to the test. According to James W. Hadley of the Lawrence Radiation Laboratory, these seismic disturbances invariably release a substantially smaller amount of energy (approximately 1 percent) than the associated test. Thus, the AEC asserts that the "natural" earthquakes which occur subsequent to an underground test are invariably of substantially less Richter magnitude than that of the associated test.

A principal concern here is that a number of seismic authorities are of the opinion that there is a significant finite probability of the test triggering an earthquake of Richter magnitude greater than the test. Egan O'Connor summarized this issue in the Cannikin Critique:

> Due to its remote location, Cannikin is worrisome not in itself as a 7.0 shock (the AEC predicted Richter magnitude of Cannikin), but rather as a trigger of something bigger.

> The triggering mechanism is not understood, but observations are that big earthquakes often begin with relatively small shocks and then trigger up to the peak intensity. But since the AEC has been recording Amchitka quakes carefully, there have been several (perhaps a dozen or so) which peaked between 6.0 and 6.6. Their triggers (or initial shocks) were smaller—for instance, the quake of September 11, 1969, began with a shock of 5.2 and triggered itself up to 6.5.

The great Alaskan quake of March 27, 1964, began with a shock of about 6.5 and peaked at 8.4.

The triggering or "lock-step" or "domino" phenomenon is well recognized by titans in seismology such as Dr. James P. Brune and Dr. Frank Press.

Cannikin will provide a trigger of 6.8 or larger.

How can the AEC say that Cannikin will provide only a "negligible" or "slight" trigger in comparison with natural triggering effects, when in fact Cannikin will be larger than any natural trigger they have ever observed in the region?

The impact of a Cannikin generated earthquake on the immediate surroundings would of course be important, however, from a worldwide point of view a more vital problem is the possibility of such an event facilitating an atmospheric or ocean leak of radioisotopes from the adjacent Longshot and Milrow test sites. Remarkably, little, if any, serious consideration of this problem arose at the Alaska Cannikin Hearings. Members of the Don't Make a Wave Committee (Patrick Moore, James Bohlen) raised this question at the Hearings: no responsible or informative reply was forthcoming from members of the AEC panel of scientists. The lack of response did, however, clearly indicate that the AEC regarded such a possibility as essentially remote. (Some indication as to the deformation capabilities of a large earthquake is given in the subsequent paragraphs.)

While consideration of the earthquake risk, *per se*, is important, it is integrally tied to the associated problem of tsunamis. Further discussion of this issue is deferred to the following section.

The Aleutian Tsunami Problem

What is a tsunami? California Senator Alfred E. Alquist (Chairman of the Legislative Joint Committee on Seismic Activity) recently described a much publicized tsunami:

On the evening of March 27, 1964, the 8.5 Alaskan Good Friday Earthquake generated a tsunami that Californian residents will not soon forget.

Damage from the earthquake occurred all along the North American coast: Alaska, British Columbia, Washington, Oregon, the San Francisco Bay area and Santa Cruz, and particularly Crescent City, California. The geography of the Crescent area helped to compound the situation when a 12-foot wave caused $11 million in damage, destroyed 27 blocks of the downtown area, and crushed over 300 buildings while miraculously causing only five deaths.

It is generally considered that destructive tsunamis are normally caused by large earthquakes, although volcanoes or submarine landslides have also generated these anomalous sea waves. Tsunamis associated with earthquakes are thought to result from vertical deformation of the sea floor over a very large area, such that the sea surface is similarly deformed, and subsequently seeks its own level as a propagating wave disturbance. The Alaska Earthquake produced measurable vertical deformation over an area of about 100,000 square miles, with the principal deformation activity in an area of about 40,000 square miles.

Dr. William C. Van Dorn of the Scripps Institute of Oceanography described the tsunami phenomenon before the Alaska Cannikin hearings:

As soon as deformed, the ocean surface disturbance begins to spread radially outward across the ocean in all directions. Initially, the wave pattern conforms to the shape of the dislocated area, but it soon becomes nearly circular, and consists of concentric rings of waves, the outermost—and longest—of which travels at about 500 miles per hour. As they travel outwards, all waves retain their identities, but their heights progressively diminish, owing to radial stretching and geometric spreading of the fixed amount of energy imparted by the source. The waves are highest in a direction perpendicular to the source axis (the fault) and lowest parallel to it. Thus, in Alaska, the principal energy was radiated southeast, along the coast of North America, and the waves traveling southwesterly along the Aleutian chain were only about half as high.

Upon entering shallow water along the continental margins, the symmetrical wave pattern becomes confused by interaction with the irregular coastline. Locally, a tsunami is manifested as a series of surges and withdrawals at intervals ranging from 10 minutes to 2 hours, depending upon the particular location. While wave intensity varies widely from point to point along the coast, its average intensity depends upon the magnitude of the source disturbance, the distance the waves have traveled, and the orientation and steepness of the offshore slope; steep slopes, such as off Hawaii and Japan, characteristically magnify wave action, gradual slopes (California and Southeastern Alaska) diminish it.

In principal, there are two ways a Cannikin generated tsunami could arise: direct generation due to the effects of the zero point cavity expansion; and, indirectly, *via* a triggered earthquake of magnitude greater of equal to 7.4. (Only earthquakes of this magnitude are known to have produced destructive tsunamis.)

The AEC asserts that the Milrow test domed the shoreline of Amchitka upwards a maximum of 8 inches for a distance of one mile. Given the relative depth of Cannikin, the doming effects are considered to be essentially that of Milrow and clearly less than the massive vertical deformation requirements for a destructive tsunami. While a direct generation of a tsunami seems unreasonable, the AEC's assurances are not as compelling as regards an indirect earthquake triggered tsunami.

AEC Deputy Director Fred R. Tesche stated at the Cannikin Hearings that seismic records indicate 20 earthquakes, equal to, or greater than, 7.75 have occurred in the Aleutian trench since 1899. Of these, 3 have resulted in recorded tsunamis, all of these seismic centers were east of Amchitka Pass. It should be noted here that the 3 in question all occurred in the last 25 years.

The origins of these 20 quakes were all along the south coast of Alaska, 5 of the 20 were west of Amchitka Pass. The epicenter of the most recent of these 5 quakes (February 4, 1965, Magnitude 7.5) was located only 20 miles Ssouthwest of Amchitka Island, and produced only a small, local tsunami.

The AEC position is that the lack of tsunami activity in the otherwise seismically active Western sector of the Aleutians suggests that earthquakes in this area are prone to horizontal rather than vertical motions.

It is interesting that the geological survey evidence cited covers an area extending westward from Amchitka some 500 miles to the end of the Aleutian chain; however, the AEC made no mention of findings or survey in the area to the immediate east of Amchitka Pass. Surely such information is critical as regards the possible generation of a destructive tsunami.

Summary

The principal issues regarding the Cannikin test are considered to be:

(1) The AEC have stated that Cannikin is essential for the ABM Basic Spartan weapon and, in turn, the national security of the U.S. and the free world. However, the Federation of American Scientists have asserted that the ABM Spartan has been rendered essentially obsolete by the development of the "Improved Spartan" missile—which does not require Cannikin. Moreover, as the FAS has indicated, President Nixon has announced U.S.-Soviet agreement to "concentrate efforts this year" (1971) on a treaty limiting ABM systems." If the envisaged agreement at the SALT talks is realized this year (1971), as expected, it is considered by many defense planners that Basic Spartan will not be required.

(2) The whole concept of developing and deploying nuclear weapons systems as a principal means of maintaining national security has

undergone a substantial re-evaluation by a significant number of the U.S. administrators, scientists and most notably by high ranking officials within the U.S. Department of Defense itself.

(3) The Under-secretaries Committee of the National Security Council have presented a detailed study to counsel the President regarding the political implications of proceeding with or canceling Cannikin. As there was no consensus, for or against, no recommendation was made by the Committee. The final decision is President Nixon's. Undoubtedly this decision will be based on purely political grounds.

(4) The AEC have stated that all, or essentially all, of the radioactive inventory of Cannikin will be contained. Critics in the scientific community indicate that the history of the AEC's underground test program has been less than desirable as regards containment. Twenty-nine percent of the AEC's underground nuclear tests at the Nevada Test Site (NTS) have leaked measurable amounts of radioactive materials.

(5) Dr. John W. Gofman, Dr. Leonard A. Walker and other eminent radiation biologists argue against the concept of "Recommended Concentration Guides," put forward by the AEC. The former have concluded that, essentially, there are no safe levels of radiation, especially when the radioactive elements under consideration exhibit long half-lives and are those known to be accumulated in biosphere food chains.

(6) Due to the initial high concentration and long half-lives of some of the radioactive elements generated by the Cannikin test, of the order of 100,000 years will be required to effect essentially complete decay of these radioactive materials. During this period, the Cannikin site, like its predecessors, will be a continuous threat to the biosphere.

(7) The Alaska State Government has expressed marked concern regarding the economic impact of a potential or actual contamination of the nearly 100 million dollar per annum Alaska fishing and shellfish industry. The State Government has indicated that a future ocean leak at

Amchitka would pose a world wide threat in regard to marketing and human consumption.

(8) The Alaska Government have also criticized the AEC as regards the impact of the Cannikin test on the biology of Amchitka Island; specifically, it is publicly stated government opinion that the AEC have significantly underestimated the impact upon sea otters, seal, sea lion, and other species populations in the area. (An interesting, if somewhat digressive consideration is the fact that as Amchitka Island is part of the Aleutian Islands National Wildlife Refuge, American Federal Law rather ironically prohibits the discharge of firearms on Amchitka.)

(9) The surrounding island communities notwithstanding, the problem of damage to principal population centers as a direct result of the seismic disturbances generated by Cannikin is regarded as minimal due to Amchitka's remoteness. However, the seismic effect upon the immediate surroundings is of paramount significance as regards to facilitating a leak of radioactive material from the adjacent Longshot and Milrow sites.

(10) There is marked public concern regarding the possibility of a Cannikin generated destructive tsunami which could clearly affect distant population centers. Alaska Senator Gravel and California Senator Alquist, for example, have pointed out that neither theory nor history are in support of the AEC's assurances regarding a possible Cannikin tsunami. Indeed tsunamis from the Aleutians have in fact caused extensive damage as far away as California and Hawaii. Seismologists indicate there is a significant probability that the Cannikin test could trigger an earthquake of sufficient magnitude to trigger a tsunami.

INDEX

ALSO PUBLISHED BY

BLACK
ROSE
BOOKS

EVERY LIFE IS A STORY
The Social Relations of Science, Ecology and Peace
Fred H. Knelman

The theme of globalization and the nature of global change provide the context and environment of the book's analysis. Knelman first deals with the nature of science and the behaviour of scientists, using the decision to drop the atom bomb on Hiroshima in 1945 and its lasting legacy, as a case study. He then turns to an analysis of nuclear power, military and civil, and the fatal link between them. A history of environmental thought precedes a shift to the global stage—the phenomenon of global change and the challenge of global governance. The last chapter describes a model of social sustainability.

> An astute analysis coupled with profound understanding. —Roger Dittmann, United States Federation of Scholars and Scientists

> For everyone concerned with creating a better future. —David Krieger, President, Nuclear Age Peace Foundation

> A most definitive work destined to be the anti-nuclear classic of all time. —Ben Weintraub, United Nations Representative, Veterans Against Nuclear Arms

Fred H. Knelman received his doctorate in Physics and Engineering at the University of London, UK. For almost fifty years, he has been synonymous with the anti-nuclear and peace movements in Canada and throughout the Western hemisphere. As listed in the 1997 edition of Who's Who, Knelman is the recipient of many awards.

256 pages
Paperback ISBN: 1-55164-136-4 $24.99
Hardcover ISBN: 1-55164-137-2 $53.99

CERTAINTIES AND DOUBTS
A Philosophy of Life
Anatol Rapoport

From the world concert stage, to service in the U.S. Air Force, from journalism to mathematics, from studies in conflict and cooperation to peace research, Anatol Rapoport has been both pioneer and lead-figure. Author of approximately 500 publications, Rapoport has spearheaded many scientific innovations, including the application of mathematical methods, first to Biology and later to the Social Sciences.

Here, he recounts his life and the people he met along the way.

Anatol Rapoport represents a uniquely many-side personality. This book is interesting not only because it contains the memoirs of one of the most important scientists of our time but also it reveals the thoughts of a great humanist.

—from the Foreword of the Russian edition, by A.V. Brushlinsky, Corresponding Member of the Russian Academy of Sciences, and, L.B. Ruban, Doctor of Sociological Science

Anatol Rapoport is Professor Emeritus of Psychology and Mathematics at the University of Toronto. He has been the recipient of many awards, including the Lenz International Peace Research Prize and the Harold D. Lasswell Award for Distinguished Scientific Contributions to Political Psychology, and honorary doctorates, of Human Letters (University of Western Michigan), of Laws (University of Toronto), of Science (Royal Military College), and of Sociology (University of Bern).

208 pages
Paperback ISBN: 1-55164-168-2 $19.99
Hardcover ISBN: 1-55164-169-0 $48.99

BOOKS OF RELATED INTEREST

Anarchism and Ecology, *by Graham Purchase*

Balance: Art and Nature, *by John Grande*

Ecology of Everyday Life, *by Chaia Heller*

Evolution and Environment, *by Peter Kropotkin*

Exporting Danger, *by Ron Finch*

Fateful Triangle, *by Noam Chomsky*

Murray Bookchin Reader, *by Janet Biehl and Murray Bookchin*

Nationalism and Culture, *by Rudolf Rocker*

No Nukes, *by Anna Gyorgy and Friends*

Nuclear Power Game, *by Ronald Babin*

Perspectives on Power, *by Noam Chomsky*

Philosophy of Social Ecology, *by Murray Bookchin*

Politics of Social Ecology, *by Murray Bookchin*

send for a free catalogue of all our titles

BLACK ROSE BOOKS

C.P. 1258, Succ. Place du Parc

Montréal, Québec

H3W 2R3 Canada

or visit our web site at: http://www.web.net/blackrosebooks

To order books in North America:

(phone) 1-800-565-9523 (fax) 1-800-221-9985

In the UK & Europe: (phone) 44(0)20 8986-4854 (fax) 44(0)20 8533-5821

Printed by the workers of

MARC VEILLEUX IMPRIMEUR INC.

Boucherville, Québec

for Black Rose Books Ltd.